WADSWORTH PHILOSOPHERS SERIES

ON

FREGE

Joseph Salerno
Texas A&M University

WADSWORTH

THOMSON LEARNING

Australia • Canada • Mexico • Singapore • Spain
United Kingdom • United States

For Berit

Printed in the United States of America
1 2 3 4 5 6 7 04 03 02 01 00

For permission to use material from this text, contact us:
Web: http://www.thomsonrights.com
Fax: 1-800-730-2215
Phone: 1-800-730-2214

For more information, contact:
Wadsworth/Thomson Learning, Inc.
10 Davis Drive
Belmont, CA 94002-3098
USA
http://www.wadsworth.com

ISBN: 0-534-58367-9

Table of Contents

Acknowledgements

I am indebted to Neil Tennant for his valuable assistance in correcting the final draft. The manuscript also benefited from comments by the editor, Daniel Kolak. My thanks to him for giving me the opportunity to write this book, and to the Department of Philosophy at Texas A&M University for the time and resources to complete the project. I am grateful to William Taschek for sparking my interest in Frege's philosophy. My deepest gratitude is to Berit Brogaard, not only for reading the manuscript and providing valuable comments, suggestions, and criticisms, but for being a great philosophical inspiration. It is to her that this manuscript is dedicated.

Preface

The following is an introduction to the philosophy of language and philosophy of logic developed by Gottlob Frege. He is well known for having defended the idea that linguistic meanings are neither physical nor psychological entities, but instead are of their own kind occupying a third realm of objective and mind-independent reality. With the objectivity and mind-independence of meaning, we will develop Frege's account of the objectivity and mind-independence of thought, truth and the laws of logic. Philosophers seldom grapple systematically with these Fregean themes prior to graduate school owing to the difficulty of the subject matter. This book was written to overcome that obstacle, and so, to make Frege's very influential ideas accessible even to the beginning philosopher. The attempt here is to organize, present and clarify the puzzles, arguments, distinctions and theories found in some of Frege's most important writings on the subject of meaning. *On Frege* is intended primarily to supplement a reading of Frege's "On Sense and Reference" and "Thoughts", both of which can be found in *The Frege Reader*, ed. Michael Beaney, (Blackwell, 1997). Many other important selections can be found there as well. All translations cited in *On Frege* are taken from that volume, unless otherwise specified. In most cases the page numbers from Frege's original publications are cited. These numbers can be found in the margins of many Frege translations, and so, the student utilizing this book is not restricted to reading the translations preferred herein.

1
Biography

Gottlob Frege (1848-1925) was a German born mathematician passionately absorbed in philosophical questions about the foundations of mathematics and the nature of linguistic meaning. He is often compared with Aristotle for his revolutionary advances in logic, and is hailed as the father of many disciplines: modern logic, formal semantics, philosophy of language and philosophy of mathematics. Anyone currently working in those areas must come to terms with Frege's philosophy. For he articulated with previously unparalleled clarity not only the philosophical problems that eventually defined those discipline but the methodology required to resolve them. The methodology is modern logic, his most prized invention.

Not much is known about Frege's personal life other than that it was fraught with tragedy. At the age of eighteen, he lost his father; at the age of thirty, his mother. All his natural children (if he had any at all) are believed to have died young, and his wife as well met an untimely fate.[1] Illness tormented much of Frege's remaining life. His adopted son, Alfred, outlived him, but only to be killed in war.

Frege attended the University of Jena and then the University of Göttingen, where he studied mathematics, physics and philosophy. He earned his doctorate at the age of twenty-five for his dissertation titled, 'On a Geometrical Representation of Imaginary Figures in the Plane'.

He then returned to Jena to teach, and remained there until his retirement forty-nine years later.

Frege's preoccupation with the foundations of mathematics began early in his career with his dissatisfaction with existing texts on the subject. The important mathematical concepts were often left undefined, and the basic laws left unproven. Frege's life's work was an attempt in one way or another (1) to clarify the concepts of arithmetic (such as the concepts of ordering-in-a-sequence, number and magnitude), (2) to make explicit and unambiguous the fundamental assumptions upon which all of arithmetic rests, and (3) to develop a precise notion of proof with which one may derive and strictly justify the remaining mathematical truths. Frege's doctrine, known as *logicism*, is that arithmetic is reducible to logic: arithmetical concepts may be defined purely in terms of logical ones, and the basic laws of arithmetic may be proved from the laws of logic alone.

Frege dedicated his life to the systematic development of logicism, and in the end failed to achieve his goal. The failure was demonstrated by Bertrand Russell in a short letter to Frege. Russell demonstrates the inconsistency of a fundamental assumption in Frege's theory. The assumption (listed as Axiom V in Frege's *Basic Laws of Arithmetic*) is this:

(Axiom V) a definable collection always forms a totality.

"The collection of all black cats", for instance, forms a totality of elements that are black cats. Notice that some definable collections contain themselves. "The collection of all non-cats" forms a totality of elements. And that very collection, being a non-cat, is one of the elements contained in the collection. Russell asks Frege to consider the following definable collection (call it C):

(C) the collection of all collections not contained in themselves.

Does C contain itself? Suppose not. Then C is a collection that does not contain itself. But then C contains itself, since C is the collection of *all* collections that do not contain themselves. So if C does not contain itself, then C contains itself. Hence, C does contain itself after all. But then C is not an element in the collection of all collections that *do not* contain themselves. So, if C contains itself, then it does not contain itself. In sum,

C contains itself, if and only if C does not contain itself.

This is self-contradictory, so the definable collection expressed by C does not form a totality of elements. That particular collection of elements is impossible. Russell concludes that Axiom V is false, "that under certain circumstances a definable collection does not form a totality."[2] This result is the notorious *Russell Paradox*. The paradox ultimately persuaded Frege to abandon his vision of mathematics as a branch of logic.

Trying to prove logicism, Frege made many fruitful discoveries that are widely appreciated today. He clearly differentiated between language and meta-language and articulated the use/mention distinction. He developed an unambiguous symbolic language for representing sentences and evaluating deductive inference. Integrating algebraic functions into logic, he replaced the less useful subject/predicate analysis of propositions with a more powerful function/argument analysis. He developed the theory of quantifiers and a complete account of both sentence and predicate logic. His truth-functional semantics for sentence logic, presented today in the form of truth-tables, can be found in virtually every logic book. Due to the expressive power, precision, completeness and overall usefulness of the formal system, Frege's logic has replaced Aristotle's to become the most important tool in the evaluation of deductive reasoning.

Nonetheless, Frege's most important and revolutionary discoveries were, by his contemporaries, widely misunderstood if considered at all. This was Frege's life-long disappointment, and it inspired his adversarial writing style. Frege's criticisms of opposing viewpoints purposely aimed to incite a public response. For instance, while criticizing one of his colleagues at Jena, he writes

> In the preceding essay, I have combated a theory objectively and seriously. If Mr. Thomae knows something that can be opposed to it, then it is his duty to present it. There is no valid reason for keeping it back, except perhaps for continuing weakness.[3]

And while explaining his irritation and the delay with which he had published the *Basic Laws of Arithmetic*, he mentions the reason for my delay: the discouragement that overcame me at times because of the cool reception–or more accurately the lack of reception–accorded by mathematicians to [my earlier work]. ...My only remaining hope is that someone may have enough confidence in the matter beforehand to expect in the intellectual profit a sufficient reward, and that he will make public the outcome of his careful examination. Not that only a laudatory review could satisfy me; on the contrary, I should far prefer an attack that is thoroughly well-informed than a commendation in general terms not touching the root of the matter.[4]

Frege believed that if philosophical mathematicians just took the time to work carefully through his results, they would see that he had revolutionized the study of logic and mathematics. He was right, but such care was not paid to his writings until after his death. Frege's frustration perhaps explains his pugilistic writing style.

Among the few who were moved by Frege's work in his lifetime were Bertrand Russell, Ludwig Wittgenstein and Rudolf Carnap. Many of their most important insights were deeply influenced by Frege's philosophy. It is primarily through the interest that they drew that Frege's writings finally received widespread recognition. It is also from them that we learn the most about Frege's character. In a letter Russell describes Frege's reaction to the paradox:

As I think about acts of integrity and grace, I realise that there is nothing in my knowledge to compare with Frege's dedication to truth. His entire life's work was on the verge of completion, much of his work had been ignored to the benefit of men infinitely less capable, his second volume was about to be published, and upon finding that his fundamental assumption was in error, he responded with intellectual pleasure clearly submerging any feelings of personal disappointment. It was almost superhuman and a telling indication of that of which men are capable if their dedication is to creative work and knowledge instead of cruder efforts to dominate and be known.[5]

Frege's thought was fully absorbed in logic and its proper development. He appears to have had little else to talk about with other philosophers.

Wittgenstein describes his impressionable first encounter with Frege in 1911:

> I wrote to Frege, putting forward some objections to his theories, and waited anxiously for a reply. To my great pleasure, Frege wrote and asked me to come and see him. ...I was shown into Frege's study. Frege was a small, neat man with a pointed beard, who bounced around the room as he talked. He absolutely wiped the floor with me, and I felt very depressed; but at the end he said, "You must come again", so I cheered up.
>
> I had several discussions with him after that. Frege would never talk about anything but logic and mathematics; if I started on some other subject, he would say something polite and then plunge back into logic and mathematics. He once showed me an obituary on a colleague, who, it was said, never used a word without knowing what it meant; he expressed astonishment that a man should be praised for this!

Frege advised Wittgenstein to study philosophy with Bertrand Russell at Cambridge. Wittgenstein took this advice and went on eventually to publish his now famous doctoral dissertation, *Tractatus Logico-Philosophicus*, a proper understanding of which cannot be had without a prior understanding of Frege's work.

Frege also greatly influenced Rudolf Carnap, who attended his lectures at the University of Jena. Carnap went on to be a prominent member of the Vienna Circle and advocate of Logical Positivism. Carnap began his studies with Frege in 1910, well after the death of Frege's wife and Russell's discovery of the great inconsistency in Frege's logicism. Carnap describes his teacher's manner and influence in his intellectual autobiography[6]:

> Frege looked old beyond his years. He was of small stature, rather shy, extremely introverted. He seldom looked at the audience. Ordinarily we saw only his back, while he drew the strange diagrams of his symbolism on the blackboard and explained them. Never did a student ask a question or make a remark, whether during the lecture or afterwards.

The possibility of a discussion seemed to be out of the question.

...the most fruitful inspiration I received from university lectures did not come from those in the fields of philosophy proper or mathematics proper, but rather from the lectures of Frege on the borderlands between those fields.

Little else is known about Frege's character and personal life, though it is clear that his dedication and influence upon other great philosophers was strong.

Frege's deteriorating health finally failed him in 1925. He died not knowing how powerful his influence would be. The faith that his work would one day be better understood is reflected in a note attached to his will. It was addressed to his adopted son:

Dear Alfred,

Do not despise the pieces I have written. Even if all is not gold, there is gold in them. I believe there are things here which will one day be prized much more highly than they are now. Take care that nothing gets lost.
Your loving father

The gold in Frege's writings was discovered and widely distributed by the 1960's. The following chapters are an attempt to make accessible, to an even wider audience, those philosophical ideas that generated a new era in philosophy, the era of analytic philosophy.

Endnotes

[1] There is disagreement among Frege biographers as to whether Frege had any natural children.

[2] "Letter to Frege" in van Heijenoort (ed.), *From Frege to Gödel: a Source Book in Mathematical Logic*, Harvard University Press, 1967, p. 125.

[3] "The Impossibility of Thomae's Formal Arithmetic" in B. McGuiness (ed.), *Collected Papers On Mathematics, Logic and Philosophy*, Oxford, 1984, p. 350.

[4] Introduction to *The Basic Laws of Arithmetic*, M. Furth (trans. and ed.), University of California Press, 1967, xi.

[5] From a letter to Jean van Heijenoort, in van Heijenoort (ed.), *From Frege to Gödel: a Source Book in Mathematical Logic*, Harvard University Press, 1967, p. 127.

[6] Found in *The Philosophy of Rudolf Carnap*, P.A. Schilpp (ed.), La Salle, Open Court Press, 1963.

2
Sense and Reference

Frege is best known as the author of "On Sense and Reference" (published in 1892). There he discovers that linguistic meanings are objects in their own right–that the semantic contents of thought and talk can be neither the circumstances that such thought and talk is about nor the psychological states that we associate with our thinking and speaking. Rather, on Frege's view, content is a necessary intermediary between mind and world. As such it explains the very possibility of communication about the world. Many philosophers today still find these findings useful and true. And though many others disagree with Frege's conclusions, it is clear that "On Sense and Reference" is the predominant inspiration (or provocation) for contemporary theories of meaning and reference. For this reason "On Sense and Reference" marks the birth of the Philosophy of Language as we know it today.

A Semantic Puzzle

Identity statements identify one thing with another. 'Clark Kent is the same as Superman', '2 + 2 = 4' and 'The Morning Star is the Evening Star' are all identity statements. Frege begins with some semantic questions about identity statements. Just what is it that we grasp when we grasp the meaning of an identity statement? We grasp what is being said or expressed. But does such a sentence express a relation between objects or between signs (for those objects). Does 'The Morning Star is the Evening Star' say of some object that it is identical to itself? Or does it say something about the names 'Morning Star' and 'Evening Star'? Obviously, the sign 'Morning Star' is not one and the same sign as 'Evening Star', since they are made up of different letters. Nevertheless, it is arguable that the sentence is about the signs. Perhaps, for example, the identity statement says that the names 'Morning Star' and 'Evening Star' name the same object. It is in this way that an identity claim may be thought to express a relation between signs.

So that is the question before us. Does an identity statement express a relation between objects or signs? Frege shows that, given standard philosophical resources, there are serious troubles with either answer. That is the semantic puzzle. Attempting to resolve this puzzle with his distinction between sense and reference, Frege develops a very rich philosophy of language–a philosophy that not only includes resources for solving this problem of identity but contributes deeper insights about the metaphysical nature of linguistic meaning, and how language connects us to the world. Let us turn now to a detailed analysis of the puzzle.

Consider a true statement of identity of the form a = a, such as

The Morning Star is the Morning Star.

All claims of this form are trivially true and uninformative for two very important reasons. First, we already know *a priori* (i.e., in advance of any empirical discovery) that each object is identical to itself. No new knowledge is gained by being told that the Morning Star is the Morning Star. And second, such claims are analytic (i.e., true in virtue of meaning alone). That is, merely understanding such a statement is sufficient for recognizing that it is true. Contrast this with the following:

The Morning Star is identical to the Evening Star,

or any true statement of the form a = b. Many such statements are neither *a priori* nor analytic. Knowing that the Morning Star is the Evening Star is the result of a great empirical discovery. It was only

9

after extensive observation that we would finally realize that both "stars" are the planet Venus. And apparently, such a statement is not true in virtue of meaning alone, since it seems that one can understand the statement (i.e., know what it means) without immediately recognizing that it is true. We can imagine someone considering the identity claim at some time before the discovery, fully understanding what that claim means, but without thereby recognizing it as true.

What this contrast is supposed to show is that sentences 'a = a' and 'a = b' mean different things. Or as Frege puts it, two such statements express distinct "cognitive values". After all, one statement is informative (that is, one may learn something new by being told that the Morning Star is the Evening Star) and the other is not (nothing is learned by being told that the Morning Star is the Morning Star). So these statements say different things.

The term "cognitive value" may mislead the reader into thinking that Frege believes that meanings are in the head—that they are cognitive states of the individual. But as we shall later see throughout, Frege is adamantly opposed to the psychologization of meanings. For Frege, meanings do not have a psychological nature, but are cognitive only in that they have semantic content, and so, can inform and be grasped by individual minds.

What we find thus far in our discussion is Frege's criterion of identity for cognitive values: if the two statements share a cognitive value (or say the same thing), then believing one would be sufficient for believing the other. If the thought that P is one and the same as the thought that Q, then one cannot think that P without thinking that Q, and vice versa. The earlier contrast shows us that it is possible to think that the Morning Star is the Morning Star without thereby thinking that the Morning Star is the Evening Star. The reason is that the former belief (but not the latter) is known *a priori*–that is, without empirical justification. The latter belief (but not the former) can be known only after empirical observation. Thus,

> Two sentences have the same cognitive value (or express the same thing) when and only when it is impossible to believe one without believing the other.

Pretheoretically we might say that this principle gives us a test for whether sentences share a "meaning", but it does not tell us in what their meanings consist. It does not tell us which two things are expressed by 'a = a' and 'a = b', respectively, but only that they do express different things. An adequate theory of meaning must not only help us to discern meanings, but must also say something about the nature of meaning and explain what it is about those meanings that makes them distinct. Remember that the general philosophical question is this: in what does the meaning of a statement consist? More specifically, what is it that we grasp when we understand statements of identity? On Frege's view, any answer to this question must account for the cognitive difference between true statements of the form a = a and a = b. But that is precisely the difficulty. What is it about the nature of meaning that allows our two sentences to be about the same object, and yet, enables us to see the truth of one without seeing the truth of the other?

Intuitively a statement of identity says something about objects. 'a = b' apparently expresses a sameness relation between the objects designated by 'a' and 'b'. The cognitive values of 'a' and 'b' seem to be the objects designated by those terms. For that is what we grasp when we understand the names in question–namely, the objects that bear those names. In Frege's example the value of 'the Morning Star' is the object that happens to be the Morning Star, and the value of 'the Evening Star' the object that happens to be the Evening Star. More generally, the intuitive view suggests that the meaning of a name is the reference of (or the thing depicted by) the name. But then it would follow that 'a = a' and 'a = b' (when true) had the same cognitive value. 'The Morning Star is the Morning Star' and 'The Morning Star is the Evening Star' would say exactly the same thing–namely, that the object in question is the same as itself. But we have just learned (by Frege's criterion of cognitive sameness) that these two sentences do not say the same thing, since it is possible to believe the former without believing the latter. This is a problem for the view that a statement of identity is about the objects.

Recall that to say of an object that it is the same as itself is trivially true and uninformative. What is said by 'The Morning Star is the Morning Star' is trivial and uninformative. But if it says the same thing as 'The Morning Star is the Evening Star', then this sentence should also say something trivial and uninformative. The very possibility of true but informative identity statements is called into question. But this consequence is unacceptable. Surely there are true and informative statements of identity. As Frege points out:

11

The discovery that the rising sun is not new every morning, but always the same, was one of the most fertile astronomical discoveries. Even today the reidentification of a small planet or a comet is not always a matter of course.[1]

So the semantic problem may be formulated as the question of how there can be true but informative statements of identity. Just what is it that is discovered when we discover an identity? It cannot merely be that the object in question is identical to itself, since this marks no genuine discovery.

Michael Dummett offers an interesting variation on Frege's point. He notices that if the cognitive value of a proper name consists merely in its having a certain reference, then it would be impossible to grasp the meaning of a true identity statement without immediately recognizing it as true.[2] Here is the argument: Let us suppose that

(1) the cognitive value of a proper name consists merely in its having the reference that it has.

and that

(2) to understand a term (or statement) is to grasp its cognitive value.

It follows from premise 2 that

(3) if we understand 'Morning Star' and 'Evening Star', then we grasp the cognitive value of each.

And so, from lines 1 and 3,

(4) if we understand the terms 'Morning Star' and 'Evening Star', we know the reference that each has (namely, the planet Venus).

But

(5) if we truly know the reference that each term has, then we know that they have the same reference (since the reference of each term is Venus).

12

Therefore,

> (6) it is impossible to understand the terms 'Morning Star' and 'Evening Star' without immediately recognizing that the Morning Star is identical to the Evening Star.

An analogous argument exists concerning false identity statements. The analogous conclusion is that it is impossible to understand the terms 'a' and 'b' without immediately recognizing that 'a = b' is false, when 'a = b' is in fact false. More generally, it therefore follows that

> (7) for any identity statement of the form a = b, if it is not immediately recognized whether a = b is true, then 'a = b' is not understood.

Of course the outcome expressed by line 7 is counterintuitive. Surely, it is possible to understand identity statements before they are verified or falsified. Otherwise we would not be able to *entertain* the very possibility that some identity obtains, without already knowing that it does obtain. Since this is absurd, the cognitive value of a proper name must not consist merely in its having the reference that it has.

Notice that this is a variation on Frege's criticism of the theory in question. Frege's initial point is that if statements of identity are merely about objects, then they say that some object is identical to itself. It is then unclear how a statement of identity may be true *and informative*. Dummett's point is that it appears that if statements of identity are about objects, then knowing the meaning of an identity statement is to know exactly which objects are under discussion, and so, to know immediately whether the identity statement is about one or two objects. And knowing this much would obviously be enough to know whether the identity statement is true. If the statement is about one object, then it is true. If about two objects, then it is false. But then all identity statements that are true or false are so analytically, since knowing the meaning is enough to know whether it is true. Identity statements are then uninformative in the Fregean sense, since one need not examine the world to determine whether they are true.

But again, identity statements can be informative. And so, on first pass, it appears that identity statements cannot be about objects. Perhaps they are about signs.

Frege's Early Solution

In Section 8 of his first major publication, *Conceptual Notation*, Frege recognized that informative identity statements are sometimes synthetic[3] (i.e., not analytic), that they are matters of non-trivial discovery. For this reason he argued that identity is a relation between signs, rather than a relation between an object and itself. When we discover an identity a = b, what we learn is not that an object is identical to itself but that the signs 'a' and 'b' have the same cognitive value–that they signify the same thing. We learn that 'a' and 'b' refer to the same object.

In "On Sense and Reference" Frege considers his older view only to reject it. He writes,

> What we apparently want to state by a = b is that the signs or names 'a' and 'b' designate the same thing, so that those signs themselves would be under discussion; a relation between them would be asserted. But this relation would hold between the names or signs only in so far as they named or designated something. It would be mediated by the connection of the two signs with the same designated thing. But this is arbitrary. Nobody can be forbidden to use any arbitrarily producible event or object as a sign for something. In that case the sentence a = b would no longer be concerned with the subject matter, but only with its mode of designation; we would express no proper knowledge by its means. But in many cases this is just what we want to do.[4]

The concern here is this. Whether two signs designate the same thing is arbitrary. If the sense of a term consists merely in the connection it has to a certain object, then identity is an arbitrary matter–one that depends purely on which linguistic conventions we happen to have adopted. For instance we might have just as easily chosen a different sign (something other than 'Morning Star') to signify the brightest object in the morning sky. Or it might have been the case that we never chose a name to signify that object. So if identity statements were merely *about* which signs stand for which objects, then (for this very

14

reason) the truth (or falsity) of such statements would depend merely upon which signs we have chosen to stand for certain objects. But if the Morning Star is the Evening Star, then it is true–not simply because we have chosen certain signs to represent certain celestial objects–but in virtue of some astronomical fact. And such facts about the identity of celestial objects would obtain whether we had the linguistic resources to name them or not. And they would obtain in a principled (rather than an arbitrary) way, no matter which names we had chosen.

And so it seems that identity statements cannot be about the designation of signs. The discovery of an identity would no longer be about the subject matter (say, objects in the sky), but would be about our linguistic resources. "We would express no proper knowledge" with an assertion of identity, because with them we would be unable to express anything but semantic (rather than, say, astronomical or mathematical) facts.

Frege's charge against his earlier self is that a use/mention fallacy has been committed. When we *use* a name we refer to its object, as in

Socrates was a philosopher.

When we *mention* a name, we refer to the word itself, as in

'Socrates' has eight letters.

When we confuse use with mention we get into problems. It would be wrong, for instance, to say of Socrates himself that he has eight letters, or of the name 'Socrates' that it is a philosopher. Signs cannot be philosophers, and things such as people do not have a certain number of letters. To make such a mistake is to fail to acknowledge the proper subject matter of the sentence. It is to confuse word-use with word-mention.

It appears that Frege is making this point when he criticizes his earlier analysis of identity claims. Astronomical identities are about a celestial object, and not about the signs that refer to it. The proof is that a real astronomical identity would obtain no matter which words we choose to represent it, while the corresponding referential identity (namely, that signs 'a' and 'b' have the same reference) depends essentially on our choice of signs. Therefore, the view that identities are relations between signs (i.e., the view that 'a = b' says that 'a' and 'b' share a reference) is to confuse the proper subject matter of identity statements. It is to mistake the use of 'a' and 'b' for the mention of 'a' and 'b'.

We may expose Frege's earlier use/mention confusion with Alonzo Church's Translation Test.[5] In essence the test may be administered as follows. Let us suppose, for the sake of argument, that the proper analysis of an identity statement a = b is that 'a' and 'b' designate the same object. So,

>   1. "The Morning Star is the Evening Star" just means " 'Morning Star' and 'Evening Star' designate the same object".

And notice that

>   2. "The Morning Star is the Evening Star" may be translated into German as follows: "Der Morgenstern ist der Abendstern".

Now notice that the sentence " 'Morning Star' and 'Evening Star' designate the same object" is a sentence about two English signs. So,

>   3. The sentence " 'Morning Star' and 'Evening Star' designate the same object" will be translated into German as " 'The Morning Star' und 'The Evening Star' bedeuten denselben Gegenstand".

Importantly, it must be noted that a correct translation preserves meaning. So a correct translation of a sentence may be substituted for that sentence without loss of meaning. Let us then substitute those sentences appearing in premise 1 with the two German translations acquired in premises 2 and 3. We end up with

>   4. "Der Morgenstern ist der Abendstern" just means
>   " 'The Morning Star' und 'The Evening Star' bedeuten denselben Gegenstand".

But our conclusion at line 4 is clearly false. These two German sentences cannot mean the same thing. One is about stars, and the other is about English expressions. Let us prove this using Frege's test for sameness of cognitive value (discussed earlier).

16

Recall Frege's test: two sentences have different cognitive values if and only if it is possible to believe one but not the other. Notice that it is possible for a German speaker to believe "Der Morgenstern ist der Abendstern" without believing " 'The Morning Star' und 'The Evening Star' bedeuten denselben Gegenstand". For she may not know any English, so will not have any beliefs about the denotations of English terms. Nevertheless, she may be well aware that both stars are the planet Venus. Since these sentences express distinct cognitive values, they cannot express the same thing. Statement 4 is false. Therefore, the analysis which led us to Statement 4–namely, Statement 1–must also be false. The proper analysis of an identity statement a = b must not be that 'a' and 'b' share a reference. It should not be thought that an identity statement is about its constituent signs and their designations, not without blatantly confusing the *use* of words with their *mention*.

Let us recap. We have been considering Frege's original question: are identity statements about objects or signs? As we have seen, if they are about objects then apparently they say merely that a certain object is identical to itself. But then it is mysterious how a true statement of identity may say anything informative. To treat identity claims as being about signs is to commit the use/mention fallacy, failing to allow identity statements to say anything about their proper subject matter.

The Sense-Reference Distinction

Frege's later view, as developed in "On Sense and Reference" is that identity statements are about objects, not signs. Nevertheless, true statements of the form 'a = a' and 'a = b' mean different things, because there is more to the meaning of a term than its reference.

'Morning Star' and 'Evening Star' do, in a sense, mean the same thing in that they denote the same object. But those terms express very different *ways of recognizing* the object in question. When we understand the term 'Morning Star', what we have is a way of recognizing an object–namely, look for the brightest object in the morning sky. And when we understand the term 'Evening Star', we have a different way of recognizing an object–namely, look for the brightest object in the evening sky. So, in that respect 'Morning Star'

17

and 'Evening Star' do not share a meaning. They express different ways of recognizing an object. Or as Frege puts it, such terms indicate distinct ways of "presenting" or "determining" an object. Frege calls the mode of presentation (or determination) the "sense" of a term, which is to be distinguished from its reference. Terms such as 'Morning Star' and 'Evening Star' do not express the same sense, even if they do refer to the same object. On this finer-grained view, the meaning of a proper name consists in its having both a sense and a reference.

A warning about the use of the term 'meaning' should be given at this point. Frege in his earlier work *Conceptual Notation* spoke of "conceptual content" or "propositions". We might loosely call this "meaning content". None of these clearly differentiates between sense and reference, but instead run the notions of sense and reference together. From here on we will speak either of sense or of reference, so as to reflect the new-found subtlety in Frege's philosophy.[6]

Let us flesh out the sense/reference distinction more clearly with one of Frege's mathematical examples. He writes,

> Let *a*, *b*, *c* be the lines connecting the vertices of a triangle with the midpoints of the opposite sides. The point of intersection of *a* and *b* is then the same as the point of intersection of *b* and *c*. So we have different designations for the same point, and these names ('point of intersection of *a* and *b*', 'point of intersection of *b* and *c*') likewise indicate the mode of presentation; and hence the statement contains actual knowledge.[7]

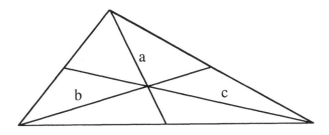

'Point of intersection of lines *a* and *b*' is an expression that denotes a point somewhere within the triangle. It is the point at which line *a*

intersects with line *b*. What we get, when we understand this expression, is a method for finding the object in question: consider line *a* and line *b*, and find the spot at which they cross paths. 'Point of intersection of *b* and *c*' is another name that denotes a point somewhere within the triangle, namely, the point where lines *b* and *c* intersect. Understanding this expression provides us with a method for finding its object: consider lines *b* and *c*, and find the spot at which they cross paths. As it turns out, the point of intersection of *a* and *b* is the same as the point of intersection of *b* and *c*. These two names pick out the same geometrical object, but they indicate different ways of finding that object.[8] That is, they denote the same reference, but do not express the same sense.

Moreover, we see in this quote that Frege believes that this new distinction is the key to solving our puzzle about identity, since he believes that with this distinction identity statements may "contain actual knowledge". Remember, the problem was to explain the possibility of true, but informative, identity statements. That is, how might 'line ab = line bc' say something non-trivial (something that can be discovered or learned), and yet be about geometrical objects (rather than geometrical signs)? In other words, we do not want our sentence

'The point of intersection of *a* and *b* is identical to the point of intersection of *b* and *c*'

to say merely that the relevant point is identical to itself. That the point is identical to itself is not informative. Yet we want that sentence to be about a geometrical point. That is, for fear of the use/mention error discussed earlier, we do not want that sentence merely to say that our *signs* refer to the same object. Geometry is not about signs; it is about points, lines, and figures.

Frege's insight is that a true identity claim may contain such "actual knowledge" when its terms share a reference but not a sense. What we discover (or know) when we discover an identity is that *the object recognizable by the first method is the same as the object recognizable by the second method.* In the geometrical example, we learn that the point determined by the intersection of *a* and *b* is the same point as that determined by the intersection of *b* and *c*. With our earlier example we learn that the celestial body recognized by looking for the brightest object in the morning sky is identical to the celestial body recognized by looking for the brightest object in the evening sky.

19

More generally, Frege's analysis explains why 'a = a' is trivial, while 'a = b' remains a matter of discovery. Or better, it explains how it is that true statements of the form 'a = a' and 'a = b' may express distinct cognitive contents. For 'a = a' just means that the object recognized by method M is the same as the object recognized by method M. This is trivially true, and known in advance of any investigation. By contrast, 'a = b' says that the object recognized by method M is the same as the object recognized by some other method M*. But it might not be known in advance that M and M* are two routes to the same object. So 'a = b' may express something that may be discovered.

Frege's analysis explains how it is possible to understand a true statement of the form a = b, without immediately recognizing it as true. For what we grasp, when we do understand the names in question, is the sense of 'a' and the sense of 'b'. And just as we may grasp several sets of directions to a location without realizing that they lead to the same location, we may grasp more than one sense without realizing that they determine the same object.

It will be useful to create a map of the terrain thus far sketched. For Frege a *sign* or a *name* is any expression that designates an object. 'Morning Star', 'Socrates', 'Plato's star pupil' and '4' are all names in this sense. The use of a proper name expresses a sense and denotes a reference.

The *reference* of a name is the object that we designate when we employ that name. Reference is "what one intends to speak of" when words are used in the ordinary way. More generally, the reference of an expression is what the expression is about.

The *sense* of a name is what is grasped when we understand the meaning of the name. Otherwise, if grasp of reference is what understanding consists in, the puzzle about the informativeness of true identity statements would remain. Moreover, and more generally, the sense of an expression is what is expressed or said when we employ it.

But what is the relation between the sense and reference of a name? As we discussed, the sense of an expression is a means for picking out a reference. The sense determines the reference.

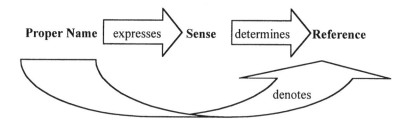

But how does the mind figure in this picture? Frege tells us that it is by using a sign that we grasp and express its sense and designate its reference. It follows from Frege's solution to the puzzle about identity statements that full understanding of an expression consists in a grasp of its sense.

But what is the nature of sense? It is natural to think of a sense as something mental, as an idea in the mind of the thinker? Frege warns against this mistake, since a sense is objective and an idea is subjective. How exactly are we to understand the difference between the subjective and the objective?

Endnotes

[1] Sense and Reference , 25-26.

[2] Michael Dummett makes this point in *Frege: Philosophy of Language*, 2nd Edition, Harvard, 1981, pp. 94-95. Michael Dummett's illuminating commentary on Frege's work fills more pages than Frege has himself published.

[3] *Conceptual Notation*, 15.

[4] Sense and Reference, 26.

[5] Alonzo Church, "On Carnap's Analysis of Statements of Assertion and Belief", *Analysis* 5, 1950, pp. 97-99. Church was a mathematical logician who rejuvenated interest in Frege's sense/reference distinction.

[6] For a clear exposition of the problems and controversies surrounding the proper translation of Frege's 'Sinn' and 'Bedeutung' (herein, 'sense' and 'reference') see Michael Beaney (ed.), *The Frege Reader*, Blackwell, 1997, pp. 36-46.

[7] Sense and Reference, 26.

[8] Frege is sometimes criticized for his choice of examples. The ones he picks lend support to his theory, but one wonders about such names as 'John' and 'Mary'. Do names of this sort really carry a sense–a way of finding the object in question? It is not clear that they do.

3
Objectivity

The Subjectivity of Ideas

In order to clarify the notion of objectivity and to see clearly why a sense has an objective nature, Frege discusses the features of those things that are stereotypically subjective–namely, ideas. First we need to ask, what is an idea? After clarifying this notion we shall determine what it is about an idea that makes it subjective. We shall then be in a position to understand the way in which a sense is said to be objective. What then is an idea?

> Even an unphilosophical man soon finds it necessary to recognize an inner world distinct from the outer world, a world of sense-impressions, of creations of his imagination, of sensations, of feelings and moods.... For brevity's sake I want to use the word 'idea' to cover all these occurrences....[1]

In the context, ideas are to be understood as internal states of the mind. They are, as Frege eventually suggests, private mental images. What distinguishes ideas from physical objects are the following four points:

1. *Ideas cannot be perceived.* Unlike a rose or a sandwich or other physical objects, we do not see, touch, smell or taste ideas. We do not discover mental images out in the world with our sense organs. They are not the types of things detectable by the senses.
2. Instead, Frege notes, *ideas are things that we have.*

> I see a green field, I thus have a visual impression of the green. I have it, but I do not see it. ...We have sensations, feelings, moods, inclinations, wishes. An idea that someone has belongs to the content of consciousness.[2]

Saying that ideas are something we have, Frege is saying something about where ideas "belong" or reside. Ideas are not out in the world, but are *internal* to the mind; one has *in one's mind* a sensation, feeling or mood. They belong to the "content of consciousness" in that they are a "part or a mode" of a conscious mind. And this claim is explicated in further detail by following points.
3. *Ideas require an owner,* someone who has them. Saying that ideas are something we have is meant to imply this further claim about what is required for the existence of an idea. An idea requires, for its existence, an owner or mind. Ideas, unlike physical objects, do not exist independently of minds. They are not in any way outside us, waiting to be detected with our sense-organs. Rather, an idea is an

> internal image, arising from memories of sense impressions I have had and acts, both internal and external, which I have performed.[3]

Internal images (ideas) arise from mental (and perhaps other physiological) processes. Importantly, such processes are causally prior to the ideas themselves. In contrast with the process of coming to know physical objects, the causal ancestry is reversed: physical objects are causally prior to the processes we use to detect them.

But these causal considerations are not enough to elucidate that which Frege is after. When he says that an idea requires an owner, he is not merely saying that ideas are the causal results of mental and physiological processes. After all, he expresses the requirement in order to contrast ideas with physical objects. Paintings and buildings, for example, are causal results of mental and physiological processes. So there must be more to the requirement than this causal consideration. It appears that ideas are dependent upon an owner, or are "mind-dependent" as we shall say, in some narrower sense.

While explaining the ownership requirement, Frege writes,

> The field and the frogs in it, the Sun which shines on them, are there no matter whether I look at them or not, but the sense-impression I have of green exists only because of me, I am its owner. It seems absurd to us that a pain, a mood, a wish should go around the world without an owner, independently. A sensation is impossible without a sentient being. The inner world presupposes somebody whose inner world it is.[4]

There is no sensation without sentience; no content of consciousness without consciousness. The claim here is that ideas cannot float around free of people who have them. Since an idea is internal to, or is a part or mode of, the mind, its existence presupposes the existence of a mind that has it. A mind is required, not only to bring ideas into existence, but also to sustain their existence. Buildings may stand long after their makers, but ideas may not. The claim then seems to be this: *the existence of an idea essentially depends on the existence of someone (or a mind) that has it.* If an idea exists, then there is some mind (or owner) which has it. Just as there is no leap without some leaping, there is no pain without someone being in pain and no feeling of anger without someone being angry.

This point is a metaphysical claim—a claim about what is necessary for the continued existence of an idea. And it is supposed to be a clarification of something that is stated in the second point already. For if it is essential to an idea that it be "a part or mode of" the mind, then clearly the existence of an ideas cannot be sustained without a mind. And conversely, if something is mind-dependent in this way, it is a part or mode of a mind.

4. *Ideas have exactly one owner.* The same idea cannot be had by more than one person. You do not have access to the contents of my consciousness, and I do not have access to the contents of yours. If I have a particular pain, you do not have that very same instance of pain. And if you have it, then I do not. Ideas are not public property. *Ideas are private.* We sometimes say things like, "I feel your pain". But we do not mean this literally. We mean that we sympathize, or know what

it is like to be in that kind of pain. Nevertheless, we do not actually have the instance of pain that somebody else is having.

The fourth point about the privacy of ideas, like the third point about mind-dependence, is supposed to follow from the second point. The second point is that an idea is something we have (i.e., essentially, something that is internal to, or part of, a mind). If a mental image, by its nature, is internal to a conscious mind, then distinct minds cannot share the same mental images. And conversely, if distinct minds can have access to the same thing, then they are not internal to a mind.

Having outlined some of the logical connections between points 2, 3, and 4, we might wonder about the following. What is their logical connection with point 1? Do any of these three points follow from the first point? That is, is it because an idea is imperceptible that it is mind-dependent and private? And does mind-dependency or privacy entail imperceptibility? Surely if a thing is publicly inaccessible, it is not perceivable by the senses. But Frege will deny the converse and claim that the imperceptibility of a thing does not imply that is publicly inaccessible. Something may be imperceptible and yet be publicly accessible, if there is some means other than sense-perception by which many people may access that thing. We will return to this discussion, since Frege argues that it is the failure of many philosophers to see this possibility that leads them to treat meanings (or senses) as mental entities. The sense of an expression, we shall see, is something that cannot be seen, touched, tasted, etc., yet is mind-independent and publicly accessible.

In the above four ways an idea differs from a physical object.[5] Ideas, unlike objects in the physical world, are imperceptible, internal, mind-dependent, and private. Perhaps ideas contribute to the meanings of our expression, in some very broad sense of 'meaning'. But ideas are stereotypically subjective, and the sense and reference of an expression, Frege demands, are objective. Frege discusses the nature of ideas, not because he has a dedicated interest in the philosophy of mind, but primarily to contrast it with the nature of sense–i.e., the objective meaning of an expression. So if we are better to understand the nature of sense and reference, it is left for us to determine which of the above features make an idea subjective.

The Objectivity of Sense

Consider the *ideational theory of meaning*, which equates the meaning of an expression with the idea normally associated with that expression. This view was developed by Modern Philosophers, such as Locke, Berkeley and Hume, and seems to have been popular among Frege's contemporaries. These philosophers did not advocate a distinction between sense and reference, so we will have to speak of 'meanings' more loosely while considering their position. Now think about the meaning of the expression 'peach'. Upon reading or hearing the expression 'peach', many of us recall from memory a visual image of the fuzzy fruit. According to the idea theorist the visual image that we call to mind is the meaning of the expression 'peach'. You understand the utterance 'peach' because you grasp that image. Likewise, most English speakers fail to understand the word 'Pfirsich' because they do not call to mind the image normally associated with its utterance.

Frege rejects the ideational theory of meaning, because the *sense* of an expression cannot be an idea:

> The idea is subjective: one man's idea is not that of another. There result ... a variety of differences in the ideas associated with the same sense. A painter, a horseman, and a zoologist will probably connect different ideas with the name 'Bucephalus'. This constitutes an essential distinction between the idea and the sign's sense, which may be the common property of many people, and so is not a part or mode of the individual mind. For one can hardly deny that mankind has a common store of thoughts which is transmitted from one generation to another. Hence it is inadvisable to use the word 'idea' to designate something so basically different.[6]

For Frege, the essential difference between ideas and senses is that the former are subjective and the latter are objective. Something is *objective*, we see, if it "may be the common property of many people"–that is, if it may be grasped or accessed by more than one person. And we see from the passage that the public accessibility of a sign's sense implies that a sense "is not a part or mode of the individual mind". Since Frege is here contrasting the subjective with the objective, we may conclude that by *objective* he means public and mind-independent. Something is subjective, if it is a part of the mind and may not be the common property of many people–that is, if it is private and mind-dependent. An idea is subjective, because (being an internal mental image) it must have one and only one owner. Such privacy and mind-dependence is at the heart of Frege's distinction between the subjective and the objective.

The important question becomes: why think that a sense must be objective? The above quote suggests that the very possibility of "transmitting" or communicating thoughts (from one generation to another) entails the intersubjective accessibility of thought. As will be discussed further in the next section, a *thought* is the sense of a whole sentence, what the sentence says or conveys. Frege correctly notes that it is impossible for a person (or generation) to convey thoughts to another, if it is not possible for both of them to grasp that which is being conveyed (i.e., if it is not possible for them to grasp the same thought). Since a person (or generation) does convey thoughts to another, many people do grasp the same thoughts. Thoughts are objective.

By arguing for the objectivity of thoughts (of the senses of sentences), Frege is in effect arguing for the objectivity of sense more generally. For he believes, and we still believe today, that the sense of a whole sentence is made up out of the senses of its constituent parts. This principle, known as the *compositionality principle*, will be defended in the next the chapter. If it is true, then one cannot grasp the sense of a sentence without grasping the sense of each constituent part of the sentence. Consequently, if the sense of 'Bucephalus' is not intersubjectively graspable, then neither is the thought expressed by 'Bucephalus died of battle wounds'. For this reason Frege need only argue for the objectivity of thoughts to make his more general point about the objectivity of sense.

Let us here sum up the argument against the claim that the sense of an expression is an idea.

> (i) If communication is possible, then sense (that which is communicated) is intersubjectively graspable.

But,

> (ii) the idea associated with an expression is private (i.e., owned by one and only one person) and idiosyncratic (i.e., different for different people).

28

The mental image that I associate with 'Bucephalus' is not identical (maybe not even similar) to the idea you associate with the word. And so, from line ii, we get

> (iii) If ideas are the senses of expressions, then sense is not intersubjectively graspable.

It follows from lines i and iii that either communication is impossible or ideas are not the senses of our expressions. Since communication clearly is possible (i.e., we do convey thoughts), the idea theory of sense must be false.

The Objectivity of Reference

Frege also rejects the general claim that the *reference* of a term is an idea.[7] He directs his criticism against the idealist. The *idealist* believes that everything that exists is an idea, that the objective world is an illusion. Tables and chairs, rocks and kangaroos–that is, all objects–are ideas in the mind of the perceiver. All of our terms, if they refer at all, refer to mental images.

The problem with idealism then is this. The reference of an expression is what the expression is about. My expression 'the moon' is then about my idea of the moon, and my expression 'the window' is about my idea of the window. And so, when I look out of my window and say 'The moon is larger than my widow', I would be saying something blatantly false. After all, my idea of the moon (i.e., the visual image I have of the moon) is smaller than my idea of the window. And this simply shows that idealism (or any theory that entails an idea theory of reference) misplaces the subject matter of our expressions.

The idealist would complain that the above criticism is unfair, since we have not treated *all* of the relevant terms as being about ideas. We must treat all of the expressions 'the moon', 'is larger than', and 'my window', as referring to ideas. In this way we are somehow supposed to get something that adds up to the proper subject matter of the sentence 'The moon is larger than my window'. The appropriate Fregean criticism is still that the idealist has misplaced the proper subject matter of the sentence. For, as we have learned, "one man's idea is not that of another". So when I tell you that the moon is larger than my window, I am talking about my ideas–ideas to which you have no access. That sentence for you is about something totally different, since the ideas that you refer to are in your head. In effect we cannot have a legitimate conversation about the moon or anything else, since our words are never about the same things. The moral is that the use of language for the purposes of communication presupposes objective reference. It presupposes that there are intersubjectively graspable objects that our talk is about.

Frege lashes out against the skeptic in the same way. The skeptic challenges us to prove that our expressions refer at all. He entertains the possibility that unbeknownst to us there is no world, that experience is an elaborate dream, that we are at every moment deceived by an evil demon, or that we are brains in vats being fed perceptual experiences through a supercomputer. If one of the skeptical hypotheses is correct, then our expressions have no objective reference. Frege's response is the same as above.[8] *Objective Reference is presupposed by the use of language.* We do not speak or think unless we intend to speak or think about something. We do not speak to each other unless we believe that we can talk about the *same* things. Therefore, it is self-defeating to use language to entertain a skeptical hypothesis. In doing so, one presupposes objective reference. Frege then does not meet the skeptical challenge by proving that there is an objective world of objects to which our terms refer. Rather he suggests that the challenge undermines itself, since all speakers (including the skeptic) presuppose objective reference by their very use of language.

The skeptic would perhaps reply by saying that presupposing objective reference does not make it exist. Maybe we *intend* to refer whenever we think or speak, but nevertheless fail to refer without realizing it. Frege admits this much. Nevertheless, his point is that we already take language seriously by using it. All speakers really do believe that it works and that it allows us to communicate about the world, otherwise we would not try to communicate. For this reason Frege is uninterested in proving that language works for the purposes of communication. It seems to work very well. What he seeks, in his life-long study of the nature and structure of meaning, is an account of *how* language works.

The objectivity of sense and reference is essential to Frege's philosophy. In this Chapter we have seen that Fregean objectivity contrasts with the subjectivity of mental images, consists in a notion of intersubjective graspability, and is intimately related to the very possibility of communication. The sense and reference of an expression are objective, if communication is possible. In the last Chapter we learned that despite the objective nature of sense, a sense is not some chunk of the world that we normally talk about. The sense of a name, for instance, is not the object that the name denotes. And the sense of a sentence (a thought) is not the state of affairs that the sentence is about. A sense is not a physical thing. But neither is it a mental entity. Senses, for Frege, are of their own kind. They furnish a third order of imperceptible, objective reality.

Endnotes

[1] Thoughts, 66.

[2] Thoughts, 67.

[3] Sense and Reference, 29.

[4] Thoughts, 67.

[5] Frege's most developed discussion of these four points is found in Thoughts, 67-68. Earlier remarks appear in Sense and Reference, 29–30.

[6] Sense and Reference, 29, including Frege's footnote.

[7] A version of the following argument appears in Sense and Reference, 31.

[8] Sense and Reference, 31-32.

4

Thoughts

An assertoric sentence is a sentence that asserts something. Let us say with Frege that a *thought* is expressed by (or stated in) such a sentence. The thought is that which is grasped when the sentence is understood. For instance,

that Bucephalus died in battle

and

that $2 + 2 = 4$

are thoughts expressed by the sentences 'Bucephalus died in battle' and '$2 + 2 = 4$', respectively. It is important to notice that the thought expressed by a sentence is different from the sentence itself. The same thought may be expressed in many different languages. That the book is yellow is a thought expressed both by 'The book is yellow' and by 'Das Buch ist gelb'. English speakers express and grasp the thought through the former sentence, German speakers through the latter. Moreover, two sentences of the same language may express the same thought, as with 'William defeated Harold' and 'Harold was defeated by William'. Thoughts are not inscriptions on a page. Thoughts are not physical things at all. But neither are they to be treated, in the context of Frege's writing, as psychological entities–despite the predominately psychological associations we have with the word 'thought'.

> By a thought I understand not the subjective performance of thinking but its objective content, which is capable of being the common property of several thinkers.[1]

Whatever exists in one's mind while thinking is subjective (i.e., is private or had by only one thinker). But what is expressed or grasped by the thinking–the thought or content–is objective, since it may be expressed and grasped by many thinkers.

We see that thoughts differ from physical objects (but resemble psychological objects such as ideas) in that they are not perceivable by any of the five senses. And they differ from psychological objects (but resemble physical objects such as planets, rocks and electrons) in that they do not reside privately in an individual mind, but instead may be accessed by many subjects. Thoughts, like physical objects, are said to be objective in this sense. In the present chapter we shall further develop an understanding of Frege's notion of objectivity as applied to thoughts.

The Sense of a Sentence

In "On Sense and Reference" Frege tells us that a sentence "contains" a thought, that the basic semantic categories are sense and reference, and that the thought cannot be the reference of the sentence that contains it. He concludes that a thought is the sense of the sentence that expresses it. Consider the following passage:

> Let us assume for the time being that the sentence has a reference. If we now replace one word of the sentence by another having the same reference, but a different sense, this can have no effect upon the reference of the sentence. Yet we can see that in such a case the thought changes; since, e.g., the thought in the sentence 'The Morning Star is a body illuminated by the Sun' differs from that in the sentence 'The Evening Star is a body illuminated by the Sun'. Anybody who did not know that the Evening Star is the Morning Star might hold the one thought to be true, the

other false. The thought, accordingly, cannot be the reference of the sentence, but must rather be considered as its sense.[2]

The main point here is this. If sentences refer at all, two sentences may have the same reference but express different thoughts. If Frege is right, then of course the thought is not the reference of a sentence. Let us unpack Frege's argument.

One may believe that the Morning Star is a body illuminated by the Sun without believing that the Evening Star is a body illuminated by the Sun. For it is possible that such a person does not know that the stars are identical, and perhaps believes that the Evening Star gives off its own light. So, by Frege's criterion for sameness of thought (discussed in the last chapter),

(i) The Morning Star is a body illuminated by the Sun

and

(ii) The Evening Star is a body illuminated by the Sun

express different thoughts. That is the first part of Frege's argument. But to show that thoughts are not the references of sentences, it must be shown further that (in such a case as this) the two sentences do in fact have the same reference.

Notice that the reference of 'The Morning Star' is the same as the reference of 'The Evening Star'. They are both Venus. And 'is a body illuminated by the Sun' has the same reference in sentence (i) as it has in sentence (ii). For 'is a body illuminated by the Sun' means the same thing (i.e., expresses the same sense) as it appears in both sentences. Since sense determines reference, sameness of sense entails sameness of reference. Even though a reference may be determined by more than one sense, a single sense always determines the same reference. So, if the subject terms of each sentence ('Morning Star' and 'Evening Star') have the same reference and the predicate terms of each sentence (both 'is a body illuminated by the Sun') have the same reference, then the references of the two sentences (if they each have reference) must be the same. The parts of our sentences are indistinguishable with respect to reference, so the whole sentences should be indistinguishable with respect to reference.

In the above quote Frege utilizes a basic principle of substitutivity: "If we replace one word of the sentence by another having the same reference, but a different sense, this can have no effect upon the reference of the sentence". In its more general form, it states that the reference of a sentence depends essentially on the reference of its component parts:

> If c is a component expression of a sentence S, and c has the same reference as c', then replacing c with c' in S will not alter the reference of S.

This principle has intuitive appeal. Reference is what an expression is about. And replacing one subject matter with that very same subject matter should not alter that which the sentence is about. For instance, replacing 'Bucephalus' in 'Bucephalus died in battle' with 'Alexander's favorite horse', we get 'Alexander's favorite horse died in battle'. Since 'Bucephalus' and 'Alexander's favorite horse' refer to the same thing, it is no surprise that are our two sentences are about the same state of affairs, i.e., have the same reference. Analogously, replacing 'The Morning Star' with 'The Evening Star' in 'The Morning Star is a body illuminated by the Sun' changes the sentence to 'The Evening Star is a body illuminated by the Sun'. But this change is not enough to change the reference of the sentence, since it is not enough to change the subject matter, i.e., that which the sentence is about. The two sentences have the same reference, if sentences refer at all.

Why think that a sentence has a reference at all? We will answer this question in the next chapter. For now it is enough to notice that *if* a sentence has a reference, the thought expressed by the sentence cannot function as its reference, but only as its sense. Let us summarize the argument:

1. Our two sentences contain different thoughts, since it is possible to believe one without believing the other.

2. Our two sentences have the same reference (if they have a reference at all), since the references of their corresponding component-expressions are the same.

3. So, the thought contained in a sentence is not the reference of the sentence.

4. Now, the basic semantic categories are sense and reference.

5. Therefore, the thought that is semantically contained in a sentence must be the sense expressed by the sentence.

The thought, then, is the sense, rather than the reference, of a sentence. A thought is expressed by a sentence and grasped by someone who understands it. But not all sentences contain thoughts in Frege's sense of the term.

The Truth-Evaluability of Thought

A thought for Frege is "something for which the question of truth can arise at all".[3] For this reason only certain sentences express thoughts.

> Sentences expressing wishes or requests are ruled out.... Only those sentences in which we communicate or assert something come into the question.[4]

A request like 'Close the door' or a question like 'Do you have the time?' does not express a thought, since it is not something for which the question of truth may arise. A thought is the sense of an assertoric sentence, one that asserts something or claims that something is true. Or more carefully, a thought is the sense of a sentence *capable of being true or false*. When I say, 'Frege died in 1925', I am claiming that something is true. Contrast this with my compound utterance, 'If Frege had children, then they died young'. Making this claim, I am not claiming that it is true that Frege had children. But I am treating 'Frege had children' as an assertoric sentence, since I am treating that which it says as being capable of truth or falsity. I am in effect claiming that *if* it is true that Frege had children, then some thing else must be true. So the question of truth arises, if only in a conditional sense. The thought that Frege had children is treated as being evaluable for truth or falsity. So 'Frege had children' is an assertoric sentence in this context, even if I am not using it to claim that Frege really did have children. Assertoric sentences express thoughts that are candidates for truth.

Calling a sentence assertoric, unlike calling one 'declarative', is not just to say something about its grammar. Declarative sentences have the grammar of a declaration, in contrast with interrogatives or imperatives which question or command, respectively. In most regions of discourse, declarative sentences are candidates for truth or falsity. I say 'in most regions of discourse' because there are exceptions. Not all declarative sentences express thoughts in the strict sense, because some declarative sentences are used in a context for which the question of truth or falsity does not arise. Fictional discourse, for instance, involves declarative sentences that do not make claims to truth. In Franz Kafka's *Metamorphosis* we find 'Gregor Samsa woke up to find himself changed into a monstrous vermin'. The sentence is declarative. It does declare something in one sense, but Kafka does not use it to make a claim to truth in the literal sense. That is, Kafka is not making a genuine assertion here. And he is not asking us to treat it as a candidate for truth. He is painting a picture, or telling a story. Perhaps he is trying to invoke in us an aesthetic reaction. Whatever the artist is doing, he is not making assertions about the world or aiming at truth in the relevant sense.

We might say then that a declarative sentence is one that describes a circumstance, but not all declaratives are used in the truth-value relevant sense. We will reserve the phrase 'assertoric sentence' for those sentences that are used in the truth-value relevant sense. Frege's study of language is purposely limited to this assertoric region of declarative discourse. And *thoughts* for Frege are the truth-evaluable things that are expressed within the assertoric practice.

Frege is strictly claiming that it is not the sentence itself, *qua* string of symbols, which may be true or false, though of course we do commonly say that a particular *sentence* is true. We correctly say, for instance, that the sentence 'Grass is green' is true. But symbols (or any collection of objects) are not the kinds of things that can be true or false. We shall evaluate this claim in a moment. But if it is correct, then saying that a sentence is true must, on Frege's view, be an abbreviated way of saying that what the sentence *expresses* (or says) is true. The sentence 'Grass is green' is true only because what it says is true. It says *that* grass is green, and

that grass is green

is a thought not a sentence. Or at least, this is how Frege is conceiving it. We may herein, and with Frege, use the abbreviated expression 'the sentence is true', but what we will of course mean is that the thought expressed by that sentence is true.

Let us return to our question. Why cannot a collection of objects be literally true or false? A string of symbols by itself (such as the raw inscription 'Grass is green') is no more capable of truth or falsity than a single symbol. Why is not the symbol 'G' truth-evaluable? It is not the kind of thing that figures in questions of truth or falsity. Why is not the combination of symbols, 'Gr', capable of truth or falsity? Because placing 'r' next to 'G' does not by itself have the power to change something that is not capable of being true or false into something that is capable of being true or false. What one gets with this addition is yet another entity not capable of being true or false; and so on, for any combination of symbols and spaces. *By themselves* additional symbols (and spaces) add nothing to the nature of the initial string of symbols that might change the string into something which aimed at the truth. Strings of signs in themselves are no more truth-evaluable than a pile of rocks. No matter how many rocks you add to the pile, you never get a candidate for truth.

What distinguishes thoughts from other kinds of things is that they are capable of being true or false. They are the primary bearers of truth-value. A proper theory of thought must explain how this is so, or at least it must not rule out the fact that thoughts have this special feature. That is, thoughts must be composed of special elements that are related in such a way as to give rise to the possibility of having a truth-value. We shall presently turn to Frege's attempt to understand this special way in which thoughts must be structured.

Let us first summarize. A thought is the sense of an assertoric sentence–a sentence that is used literally to get at the truth, or to assert something as being the case. Nothing is true (or false) that is not composed of parts specially suited for constituting a truth-evaluable entity. So sentences, *qua* syntactic strings, are not the bearers of truth-value. Whatever the details of their special nature, thoughts are the things that bear truth-values. It is the thought that is capable of being true or false. The question then becomes: what must a thought be like in order to have this essential feature? How are thoughts structured?

The Compositional Structure of Thought

The thought, or sense of a sentence, is built from the senses of the components expressions. A thought is composed or determined by its parts. Why would anyone think this?

Notice that there are potentially infinitely many sentences that can be understood, hence an infinite number of thoughts that can be grasped: that five plus one equals six, that five plus two equals seven, that five plus three equals eight, and so on. We are often introduced to new sentences–sentences that we have encountered for the first time, such as

> The Croatian skydiver drives a purple cab.

How is it possible to understand new sentences, without needing to be taught their meanings as they appear? How is possible for a finite mind potentially to understand an infinite number of them? Frege has an answer:

> It is astonishing what language can do. With a few syllables it can express an incalculable number of thoughts, so that even if a thought has been grasped by an inhabitant of the Earth for the first time, a form of words can be found in which it will be understood by someone else to whom it is entirely new. This would not be possible, if we could not distinguish parts of a sentence, so that the structure of the sentence can serve as a picture of the structure of the thought. To be sure, we really talk figuratively when we transfer the relation of whole and part to thoughts; yet the analogy is so ready to hand and so generally appropriate that we are hardly even bothered by the hitches which occur from time to time.[5]

The thought about the Croatian skydiver, before I expressed it, had probably never been grasped by anyone on Earth. Yet you are able to grasp it once I put it to words. How did you do that? Frege's answer seems to be that the structure of the sentence (the arrangement of the parts of the sentence) serves as a "picture" of the structure of the thought (the arrangement of the parts of the thought). Already understanding how the parts of that sentence function, you grasp the *parts* of the new thought. That is, you grasp the constituent senses that compose the new thought. The arrangement of the parts of the new sentence suggests the structure of the new thought. That is, it suggests how those constituent senses are to be related so as to form the new thought (i.e., to form the sense of the whole sentence).

More simply, the thought expressed by a sentence is the sense of the sentence. And a complex sense, such as a thought, is a function of its more basic parts. If you grasp the parts and the way in which they relate to one another, then you grasp the whole. For example, to grasp the thought that the cab is purple, you need only grasp the senses of 'the cab' and 'is purple' and know how these senses relate to one another. The sentence 'The cab is purple' suggests how these senses are to be related. In this way one is able to grasp newly introduced sentences, and a potentially infinite number of them. Frege believed that the compositional nature of thought best explains this linguistic ability. The structure of a sentence gives us a "picture" of the structure of its thought.

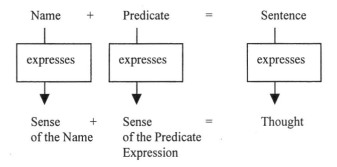

This diagram is slightly misleading, since thoughts (*qua* truth-evaluable entities) cannot be composed by a simple process of addition. As we noted in the last section, adding non-truth-evaluable things to more non-truth-evaluable things gives us nothing more than a larger collection of non-truth-evaluable things. The sense of a name and that of a predicate are not simply joined to give rise to a thought. As we see in the next section, they stand in a much more interesting relation to one another. Nevertheless, the diagram captures the idea that we grasp thoughts through the use of language. Through our use of language, we grasp the senses of names and predicates. Upon seeing or hearing new sentences that combine these terms in various way, we are able to grasp an indefinite number of new thoughts.

As with the reference of a sentence, the sense of a sentence (or thought) may be understood compositionally. The compositionality of thought may be expressed with the following substitutivity principle:

If c is a component expression of a sentence S, and c expresses the same sense as c', then replacing c with c' in S will not alter the sense of S.

'Mark Antony's last lover' and 'the last lover of Mark Antony' express the same sense. So it is no surprise, given the compositionality of thought, that 'Mark Antony's last lover killed herself' and 'The last lover of Mark Antony killed herself' express the same thought. It should be just as unsurprising to realize that 'Cleopatra killed herself' and 'Mark Antony's last lover killed herself' express distinct thoughts. This realization (which is based on the compositionality principle) corroborates the results of Frege's basic test for the sameness of thought, since it is possible to believe that Cleopatra killed herself without believing that Mark Antony's lover killed herself. This is possible, of course, if it is not known that Cleopatra was one and the same person as Antony's final lover. Distinctness of thoughts can then be explained by differences among the senses of the component expressions, and sameness of thoughts can be explained by sameness of the senses of component expressions.

Given the compositionality of thoughts, a thought is determined by its constituent parts. But what exactly are the parts of which a thought is composed? What is the sense of a name and the sense of a predicate? How do they combine to create something that is capable of being true or false, a thought? How do the parts of a thought contribute to the whole?

The Function-Argument Analysis

A thought is determined by its component parts. A thought is the sense of a sentence, and its relevant parts are senses of constituent terms of the sentence. These parts are, for instance, the sense of a name and the sense of predicate, as in

'Socrates is wise'.

The thought expressed by this sentence is composed of the sense of the name 'Socrates' and the sense of the predicate 'is wise'. Now a thought is something capable of being true or false. So whatever are to be the sense of a name and the sense of predicate, they had better be of a kind to give rise to such truth-evaluability. We learned in the section on truth-evaluability that a sentence is not the thing capable of being true or false, because putting a name together with a predicate does not by itself create something capable of being true. A string of symbols plus a string of symbols only yields a larger string of symbols. Let us consider a theory of meaning that Frege criticizes for failing to account for the truth-evaluability of thoughts in this same way. We will then be a better position to see why a theory of sense is better suited to explain the essential truth-evaluable character of thought.

Consider once again the ideational theory of meaning, which claims that the meaning of a term is the idea associated with the term. This theory would have us believe that the meaning of 'Socrates' is our idea of Socrates, and the meaning of 'is wise' is our idea of wisdom. The meaning of 'Socrates is wise' must then be some composition of these two ideas. But what do we get when we put the one idea up against the other? We get two ideas. Two ideas are no more truth-evaluable than one. The point is that things that are not truth-evaluable do not give rise to truth-evaluability in virtue of their being collected. Of course, one might argue that we have failed to take into account all of the relevant ideas. There is not only the idea of Socrates and the idea of wisdom, but also the idea we have of *is*. But then we are left with a collection of three ideas: the idea of Socrates, the idea of wisdom and the idea of is. There is still no sign of anything capable of being true or false. Placing in one's mind the is-idea between the Socrates-idea and wisdom-idea does not does not serve as semantic glue. Adding mental images does not turn a set of ideas into a thought any better than does adding pictures to a gallery. We just get more pictures.

The same criticism is raise by Frege against any theory of meaning that treats the terms uniformly. If the name and the predicate both express things that are *of the same kind*, then putting those things together by addition cannot yield something for which the question of truth arises.

Let us return to Frege's theory of sense. On this view a name and a predicate-expression have a sense, but express two very different kinds of senses. The sense of a name is "complete", whereas the sense of a predicate is not. This difference, once properly understood, is meant to explain the truth-evaluable character of thoughts. Frege borrows from algebra the function/argument distinction, and applies it to analyze the semantic features of sentences more generally. Consider the following function:

$$2 + x = 5.$$

In this expression x is a place-holder for a numeral. Until that numeral is plugged in, the formula expresses an incomplete sense. The formula says that

Two plus ( ) equals five.

Functions have this incomplete nature. They have "holes", or are "unsaturated". What fills the hole, or saturates, a function is *an argument*. In this case we may plug into the expression a numeral. When we replace x with '2' or '7', the formula expresses a complete sense.

Frege treats the sense of a predicate-expression as a function and the sense of a name as an argument. The predicate 'is wise' expresses a sense that happens to be an incomplete entity; it has a hole in it. It might better be rendered as

( ) is wise.

Since a predicate-expression aims to predicate (or ascribe a property to an object), '( ) is wise' is incomplete. The function expressed here is waiting for an argument to "saturate" it. When a name is plugged into this expression, the sense of the name saturates the function to complete the thought (in this case, to complete the predication).

Let us clarify this notion of "completeness" or "saturation". The sense of an expression is *incomplete* or *unsaturated* when it is in need of further sense to complete its job. The job of a name is to name an object. 'The teacher of ( )' is an incomplete name. If we plug in 'Plato', the sense of the name is complete. It succeeds in picking out the object that is Socrates. 'Socrates', on the other hand, expresses a complete sense all by itself, because it is in no need of further sense in order that it may name an object. The job of a predicate-expression is to predicate something of, or ascribe a property to, an object. '( ) is wise' is incomplete, since it aims to predicate wisdom to something but fails to do so until it is saturated with a name. The job of a relational expression is to relate two or more objects in some way. '( ) was the teacher of ( )' aims to express a teacher/student relation between two objects. It is unsaturated until it does so. Once filled with two names, such as 'Socrates' and 'Plato', the expression succeeds in relating two objects, since it will then say that Socrates was the teacher of Plato. An argument, such as the sense of a name, is complete because it has completed it job of naming. A function, such as the sense of a predicate or relational expression, is incomplete, because it needs to complete its job of predicating something of an object or of relating two or more objects.

In the chapter on Sense and Reference we discussed the sense of a name as a "way of determining an object". What does this have to do with the function/argument analysis? How are we to understand a "way of determining an object" as the argument of a function? How are we to understand it as a "complete" sense? Consider the following expression:

$$2 + 1.$$

It expresses something complete, since it succeeds in doing its job. It is supposed to name something. It is in no need of further sense, in order that it may name an object. It already names an object, the number three. The sense of a name is complete. Notice that this expression provides a way of picking out or determining the number 3, just as 'Morning Star' or 'brightest object in the morning sky' provides a way of picking out Venus.

The sense of a name, unlike a function, is complete or saturated. It is not waiting to be filled with anything. It is said to succeed in picking out an object. With '2 + 1' we are given way of picking out the number three. With 'Morning Star' we are given a way of picking out Venus. With 'Socrates', the man that it picks out is Socrates. A way or method for picking out an object is the sense of a name. It is what we grasp when understand the name. It is complete when it succeeds in picking out an object. It completes a predication and yields a thought, when it is attached to the sense of a predicate expression.

When the sense of a predicate expression takes the sense of a name, it yields a thought. It yields something capable of being true or false. We may plug our mathematical name '2 + 1' into the function discussed earlier. Our earlier function was '( ) when added to two equals five', or '2 + x = 5'. Replacing x with '2 + 1' produces

$$2 + (2 + 1) = 5,$$

which completes the predication and yields a complete mathematical thought. And when the function expressed by 'is wise' takes the sense of 'Socrates' as its argument, it completes the ascription of wisdom to an object and yields a complete thought in the same way.

In this way Frege believes that we have begun to explain the essentially truth-evaluable nature of thought. The semantic value of a predicate is an unsaturated sense, a sense that by its nature "waits" for completion. Less metaphorically, the sense of a predicate-expression aims to predicate, or ascribe a property. But by itself it never tells us which object to ascribe the property to. Until it is said which object has the property, the predication is incomplete. That is, such an incomplete expression is in need of further sense, if it is to serve its fundamental purpose of property-attribution. So, if you take an incomplete predication and plug it up with something that completes it, the result of course will be a complete predication. And a complete predication just is something that is capable of being true or false.

Recall that the ideational theory of meaning could not explain the truth-evaluable nature of thoughts, because it is not clear how putting the idea of Socrates next to the idea of wisdom provides us with the thought that Socrates is wise. All it seems to provide is a collection of mental images. The theory of sense, on the other had, differentiates between the nature of senses. Some act like functions and others like arguments. Given the saturated versus unsaturated nature of arguments and functions, respectively, we have an explanation of how senses may combine to yield something capable of being true or false.[6]

Thoughts are the primary bearers of truth-value. So their parts must combine to create something capable of being true. With this in mind we get a much clearer perspective on the nature of sense. *The sense of an expression is the contribution it makes to the truth-evaluability of the thought of which it is a part.* The sense of a name contributes by being a means with which we may determine an object. The sense of a predicate contributes by being a means with which we may determine the predication of a property. The means for determining an object once combined with the means for determining a predication yield the thought that that object has that property. And whether that object has that property is something for which the question of truth can arise. In this way the sense of an expression is said to contribute to the truth-evaluable nature of thoughts.

Moreover, *any part of the meaning of an expression that does not contribute to the truth-evaluability of the thought is not part of the expression's sense.* Ideas cannot be the senses of our expressions, because they fail to contribute in this way. Mental images do not combine to create a new kind of thing capable of being true. They combine only to create collections of ideas.

We are now in a position to develop the sense in which a thought is said to be objective. We have already mentioned that a sign's sense is objective in that it is publicly accessible and mind-independent (not part of an individual mind). A thought, understood as essentially truth-evaluable, may be understood to be objective in a further sense.

The Objectivity of Thought

There are many senses in which a thought is said to be objective or mind-independent. Let us review and develop these ideas further.

> 1. Thoughts do not reside privately in an individual mind, but are intersubjectively accessible (i.e., the same thought may be grasped and expressed over and over again by many different minds).

> 2. Thoughts exist independently of individual acts of thinking (i.e., thinking neither causes a thought to come into existence nor sustains its existence, but exists whether we think it or not).

> 3. The truth (or falsity) of a thought is independent of our taking it to be true (or false). That is, a true thought would be true, even if we took it to be false and even if we never entertained the thought at all.

We consider each of these notions in turn.

1. *Thoughts are intersubjectively accessible.* This thesis is at the heart of Frege's more general theory of objectivity. Frege begins with the apparently uncontroversial view that the communication of thoughts is possible. His work may then be understood as an attempt to explain this possibility. Communication is an activity that includes, among other things, the ability to say that something is true and to

convey to others what is meant, and the possibility of a listener agreeing or disagreeing with what is said. But none of this can occur, if thoughts are subjective–that is, if thoughts are internal mental states.

2. *Thoughts are mind-independent; they do not depend for their existence on thinking.* This means at least two things: (a) thoughts are not to be identified with individual acts of thinking, and (b) thoughts are not to be taken to depend on acts of thinking. Let us begin with the first. Frege tells us,

> By a thought I understand not the subjective performance of thinking but its objective content, which is capable of being the common property of several thinkers.[7]

> It may well be the case that people sometimes understand by the word 'thought' an act of thinking–in any case this is not always so–and such an act cannot be true.[8]

A thought then cannot be the subjective act of thinking, because thoughts and subjective acts of thinking are essentially different. The same thought may be had by several different thinkers, while the subjective act of thinking is private or "owned" by exactly one thinker.

Moreover, thoughts are capable of truth or falsity. For this very reason it is meaningful to ask of a thought whether it is true or false. But, acts of thinking are not capable of truth or falsity. They are not suited for such semantic valuation, because they are not composed of parts which may give rise to this special feature. It is therefore not meaningful to raise the question of truth or falsity of a subjective state (or collection of subjective states). For these reasons, Frege prohibits the identification of thoughts with subjective acts of thinking. That is, thoughts, unlike subjective acts of thinking, are publicly accessible and truth-evaluable.

Neither can a thought be brought into existence by subjective acts of thinking:

> A person sees a thing, has an idea, grasps or thinks a thought. When he grasps or thinks a thought *he does not create it* but only comes to stand in a certain relation to what already exists–a different relation from seeing a thing or having an idea.[9]

47

When we see a thing (a physical object), we perceive it with one of the five senses. But neither thoughts nor ideas are physical objects, and so cannot be accessed in this way. In this respect thoughts and ideas are alike. They are not discoverable by the sense.[10] So how do we access ideas and thoughts? When we have an idea, we are aware of it purely by introspection, or (borrowing Kant's terminology), Frege says, by pure intuition.[11] But grasping a thought cannot be like this activity either, according to Frege, since introspection provides one only with the private and incommunicable contents of one's own mind. And thoughts are communicable and accessible by more than one mind.

The question still remains: why cannot thoughts be "created" or "produced" by subjective acts of thinking? One answer seems to rest on the difference between the way we access thoughts and the way we access our own mental states. If our own mental states (such as ideas, and acts of thinking) are private and incommunicable but thoughts (i.e., that which we assert to be true or false) are intersubjectively accessible and communicable, then thoughts do not depend for their existence on the mental states of the thinker.[12] In other words, nothing subjective can bring into existence anything objective.

But the argument must amount to more than this. Notice, after all, that subjective things sometimes do contribute to the existence of objective things, since a person's subjective desire to paint, for example, may bring about the existence of real paintings which are appreciable by many. But notice that in this example, the desire to paint is not the only causal factor in play. There are also the brush strokes, which are not subjective. So, if Frege believes that the subjective cannot give rise to the objective, there must be a more specific assumption implicit in his writing–namely, if a set of things causes an object x to exist and *every one of those things is subjective*, then x must also be subjective. It is perhaps implausible to think that subjective things alone can bring into existence something objective. If so, then it is implausible to think that subjective acts of thinking alone can produce thoughts.

The preceding argument concludes that thoughts are causally independent of thoughts. There is another argument more closely tied to the notion of mind-independence discussed in our Chapter on Objectivity. There we utilized the following notion of mind-dependence: x depends on the mind when the existence of x presupposes the existence of a mind that has x. So

> if x exists, then there is a mind that has x.

In that context we were contrasting the mind-dependence of an idea with the mind-independence of a sign's sense. The difference was that a sign's sense, unlike an idea, does not require the existence of a conscious mind to have it. In the present context, the question is not whether a thought requires a mind for its existence, but whether it requires acts of thinking more specifically. So let us modify our notion of mind-dependence appropriately. Let us express the dependency of a thought on an act of thinking in the following way:

> if a thought T exists, then there is an act of thinking that expresses it.

Frege rejects this kind of dependency of thoughts on thinking in the following passage:

> [w]e cannot regard thinking as a process which generates thoughts. It would be just as wrong to identify a thought with an act of thinking, so that a thought is related to thinking as a leap is to leaping. This view is in harmony with many of our ways of talking. For do we not say that the same thought is grasped by this person and by that person? And that each person has the same thought over and over again? Now if thoughts only came into existence as a result of thinking or if they were constituted by thinking, then the same thought could come into existence, cease to exist, and then come into existence again, which is absurd. As I do not create a tree by looking at it or cause a pencil to come into existence by taking hold of it, neither do I generate a thought by thinking.[13]

The claim is that if thoughts depend on thinking for their existence, then the relevant thought would fail to exist whenever the corresponding act of thinking was not occurring, just as a leap would not be in existence unless someone was leaping. Moreover, just as each act of leaping gives rise to a new leap, so too would each act of thinking give rise to a new thought. But this would make it impossible for two people to share the same thought (and so to communicate), and impossible for one person to entertain the same thought over and over again. This is absurd, given the essential nature of thoughts *qua* communicable and intersubjectively graspable objects. So we see once again an argument for the mind-independence of sense, in this case the mind-independence of thought, resting on the intersubjective accessibility of thought. Thoughts are publicly accessible, so they are mind-independent. Frege's notion of objectivity then includes, not only this notion of intersubjective graspability, but the notion of mind-independence. And there is a further sense in which thoughts are said to be objective.

3. *The truth (or falsity) of a thought is independent of our taking it to be true (or false).* In other words, a thought may be true even if we do not take it to be true.

> A law of nature is not invented by us, but discovered, and just as a desolate island in the Arctic Ocean was there long before anyone had set eyes on it, so the laws of nature, and likewise those of mathematics, have held good at all times and not just since they were discovered. This shows us that these thoughts, if true, are not only true independently of our recognizing them to be so, but that they are independent of our thinking as such.[14]

In other words, some things are true that we do not yet recognize to be true. It was true that the Arctic Ocean was there before that water was found, and $E=mc^2$ was not invented but discovered by Einstein. It was true before he published on relativity. The fact that it was true best explains why Newtonian mechanics could not explain all of the planetary motions. The point is that something can be true before we think so, and before we entertain the possibility of its being true.

Moreover, a thought may be true, even if we take it to be false. We can make mistakes. If we took it to be false that $E=mc^2$, then $E=mc^2$ would remain true. Earth would be the third planet from the Sun even if we all believed that it is was the second. This point is not very controversial. We think that truth is something that we may or may not attain. There is what we believe, and there is what is true. We hope that our beliefs align with what is true and sometimes do our best to get at the truth, but we admit that our beliefs may fall short of the truth. Such modesty is not hard to come by. But it is not Frege's opinion merely that it would be immodest to think that truth depends on, and is determined by, belief. It is conceptually mistaken:

being true is different being taken to be true, whether by one or many or everybody, and in no case is to be reduced to it. There is no contradiction in something's being true which everybody takes to be false. ... if it is true that I am writing this in my chamber on the 13th of July, 1893, while the wind howls out-of-doors, then it remains true even if all men should subsequently take it to be false.[15]

If the concept of truth were reducible to the concept of what-is-taken-to-be-true, then there would be a contradiction in thinking that something might be true but not taken to be true. Yet there is no contradiction in the thought "it would be true that the Earth is round, even if everyone believed otherwise". If truth were reducible in this way, then this thought *would* involve a contradiction. It would say,

> It would be believed by everyone that the Earth is round, even if everyone believed otherwise.

This is self-contradictory. It would not make sense to entertain the thought "it would be true that ..., even if everyone believed otherwise". But since it does makes sense to entertain the possibility of something's being true that everybody disbelieves, the concept of truth must not merely be the concept of what we take to be true.

Our very use of the term 'true' carries with it an understanding of the distinction between attempting to get it right and actually getting it right. Competent use of the truth-predicate presupposes a difference between mistaken belief and correct belief. Frege proposes that it is paradoxical to think otherwise:

> If anyone tried to contradict the statement that what is true is true independently of our recognizing it as such, he would by his very assertion contradict what he had asserted; he would be in a similar position to the Cretan who said that all Cretans are liars.[16]

This Cretan is in a precarious position. His utterance has no authority, because it undermines itself. If all Cretans are liars, then the speaker (being a Cretan) is a liar. So, what he says is not true. He says that all Cretans are liars. But then it is not true that all Cretans are liars. His

51

very claim has turned around to falsify itself. A similar outcome allegedly follows from claiming that truth is dependent on belief. Let us call this dependency thesis 'subjectivism', and someone who believes it a 'subjectivist'. The subjectivist believes,

> a thing is true when someone believes it.

Suppose that this is right. Then whether that thought is true depends on whether someone believes it. The subjectivist believes it, so it is true. But do we all recognize this principle as true? No. I believe that it is false. On the subjectivist view, then, it follows that it is true that the principle is false. After all, someone believes that it is false. But then the principle is both true and false. A contradiction follows from the subjectivist's principle. So, the principle must be false. The subjectivist's principle undermines itself. Therefore truth is independent of belief.

The above argument against subjectivism rests on the *law of non-contradiction*. This is the principle that a thought cannot be both true and false. Normally, if someone tells us that something is both true and false at the same time, we think that they are mad. But there appear to be exceptions. Suppose John says sincerely, "I love her, but I hate her". People sometimes say this truthfully. And so it would follow that it is both true and false that John loves her. But of course this means that he loves her in one sense and hates her in another sense. But if the statements have the same sense, they must have the same truth-value. Similarly for sentences containing indexicals such as 'I' or 'This'. 'I am in Texas' expresses something that is true when I utter it, and false when someone utters it outside the borders of Texas. But then my utterance and your utterance have a different sense. 'I' picks out me when I use it. It picks out somebody else when somebody else uses it. But then 'I' must not have the same sense when different people use it, since the same sense will always pick out the same object. And so, by compositionality, 'I am in Texas' expresses a different thought when different people utter it. The same thought, on the other hand, cannot have two different truth-values. The apparent cases where a thought can be both true and false, are *merely* apparent.

Frege even goes so far as to suggest that thoughts are absolutely true or false. The same thought will always have the same truth-value. On first glance this appears to be wrong, since it appears that I may express a thought now and later, thereby changing the truth-value. My thought that 'I am in Texas' may be true now, but when I express it outside of Texas it becomes false. Frege insists that 'I am in Texas' expresses a different thought depending on where you are and when you utter it. My current utterance expresses that I am in Texas now (September 1, 2000). Uttered later, the sentences would say something else, because it would be indexed to a new time. So, 'I am in Texas', if it is true, remains true. It is absolutely true.

So the fact that the same grammatical sentence is sometimes said to be true and sometimes said to be false does not show that thoughts may be both true and false or that they may change their truth-value. But then the truth of a thought does not depend on a person's thinking it true. Subjectivism is false, and a true thought is true independently of whether someone thinks it is true.

The subjectivist would be unimpressed with the above argument which utilizes the *law of non-contradiction*. This logical law denies that a thought may be both true and false, but subjectivism obviously allows for the joint truth and falsity of a thought. It allows for such just as long as one person believes something to be true and another person believes that very same thing to be false. For, on the subjectivist's view, a claim is true just as long as someone believes it. The reasoning of the above argument seems then to presuppose, rather than prove, that subjectivism is wrong. But this only puts into focus the more important reason for thinking that subjectivism is false. We shall address the issue here and in a later chapter on logic.

If it is possible for the very same thought to be both true and false, there is no possibility of a mistake in thinking. As long as somebody thinks the thought, it is true. And if one person thinks it, and the other person "contradicts" it, they are both correct. But really this is simply to deny that there is a question of correctness. For if there is nothing that it is for someone to be mistaken in judgment, then there is nothing that it is for someone to be correct. To suppose that someone could get it right presupposes that there is something that it would be for someone to get it wrong. And that is just what the subjectivist in effect denies–that one could make a mistake in judgment. The impossibility of mistake has several devastating consequences for our logical practices. Frege elaborates,

> If something were true only for him who held it to be true, there would be no contradiction between the opinions of different people. So to be consistent, any person holding

this view would have no right whatever to contradict the opposite view; he would have to espouse the principle: *non disputandum est.*[17]

When opinions contradict one another, we have a disagreement. And to have a genuine disagreement, one opinion must be the denial of the other. To deny what somebody is saying is to say that he is mistaken. So it makes no sense for people to try to disagree, unless at least one of their opinions may be mistaken. Since, on the view we are considering, there is no possibility of a mistake, it makes no sense for people to try to disagree. A clash of opinions is impossible. The very practice of disputing an issue on logical grounds is undermined.

Moreover, if opinions cannot stand in the logical relation of denial with each other, then there is no clear sense in which one opinion may be said to corroborate or affirm another. Opinions cannot agree, unless there is something that it would be for them to disagree. The very practice of agreeing with another is undermined.

The damage of subjectivism does not end there. If opinions cannot contradiction or corroborate, and one has no right to try to agree or disagree with another on logical grounds, then

> He would not be able to assert anything at all in the normal sense, and even if his utterances had the form of assertions, they would only have the status of interjections–of expressions of mental states or processes, between which and such states or processes in another person there could be no contradiction.[18]

If somebody asserts a sentence but the thing expressed cannot stand in logical relations of affirmation and denial, then the assertion has a very particular nature. It serves as the expression of something that does not stand in logical relations to other things. Interjections are like this. When someone says 'Wow!' or 'Yummy!' they express excitement or delight. They express a subjective state that does not stand in logical relations of affirmation or denial. If you say 'Yummy' and I say 'Yucky', we do not really disagree about anything. We are simply venting different sensations of taste. Our tastes are not in contradiction with one another in the logical sense, since my sensation is not the denial of yours. The disgust I feel is not a denial of the pleasantness that you feel. And my interjection 'Yucky' certainly does not say anything about your feeling. If these interjections say anything at all, they say something only about the subjective states of the person interjecting. Consider,

> YOU: 'The soup is yummy.'

> ME: 'No, it's not; it's yucky.'

Perhaps you are saying that you do not like the soup, and I am saying that I do. We are not disagreeing, since you are not really affirming anything that I deny. The soup is good to you, and the soup is bad to me. There is no contradiction here. There are no logical relations between your subjective feeling of pleasantness and my subjective feeling of disgust.

Now if the subjectivist is right, then all assertions appear to have the status of interjections. If our assertions express nothing that may stand in logical relations to one another, our assertions would be in the same boat as these interjections. When I say 'Roses are red', my utterance may amount to no more than the expression of some inner state that I have. At best, I am saying that it is true for me that roses are red. When others say 'Roses are not red', they are not saying anything about my inner state, they are not contradicting me, they are merely venting their own inner state. At best they are saying that it is true for them that roses are not red. On this view, no one person's opinion is any more justified than anyone else's, and one must admit that the opposite view is no less correct than one's own. Nobody would be able to assert anything in the "normal" sense, because there would be no authority whatsoever in the assertion. This goes as well for the subjectivist's assertion that subjectivism is true. The subjectivist must admit that asserting, 'Subjectivism is false', is no less correct. His position undermines its own authority along with the authority of any assertion.

Most importantly, subjectivism does violence to the very possibility of communication. The possibility of communication presupposes that we may share an understanding of our utterances. But if all you may express are your subjective states, then since I cannot grasp your subjective states, I cannot grasp that which you are expressing. You and I cannot really share an understanding of any of our utterances. People cannot communicate. Therefore, since communication really is sometimes successful, subjectivism must be false.

Assertions are then the expressions of thought. Thoughts are objective in that they are publicly accessible, mind-independent, and have their truth-values independently of what we think. That is the way it must be, it seems, if we are able to assert anything at all in the "normal sense"–that is, if we are able to agree, disagree and communicate. It seems clear that we are able to do this. If you disagree, you have only granted Frege his point.

Endnotes

[1] Sense and Reference, 32, footnote.

[2] Sense and Reference, 32

[3] Thoughts, 60.

[4] Thoughts, 62.

[5] *Logical Investigations*, P. T. Geach (ed.), Yale University Press, 1977, p. 55.

[6] For discussions about the nature of a function and related issues, see Frege's "Function and Concept" and "Concept and Object", both found in M. Beaney (ed.), *The Frege Reader*, Blackwell, 1997.

[7] Sense and Reference, 32, footnote.

[8] Logic (1897), posthumous fragment, 147.

[9] Thoughts, 69, footnote. [emphasis added]

[10] Thoughts and ideas are 'not real', as Frege sometimes puts it. By 'not real' he does not mean to deny their existence, but only to deny that they are discoverable by the senses.

[11] See, for instance, §26 of *The Foundations of Arithmetic*, J. L. Austin (tr.), 2nd ed., Northwestern University Press, 1980.

[12] Such an interpretation of Frege's argument may be found in Chapter 4 of Wolfgang Carl's *Frege's Theory of Sense and Reference*, Cambridge University Press, 1994.

[13] Logic (1897), 148-149.

[14] Logic (1897), 145.

[15] *The Basic Laws of Arithmetic*, M. Furth (trans. and ed.), University of California Press, 1967, xv-xvi.

[16] Logic (1897), 144.

[17] Logic (1897), 144.

[18] Logic (1897), 144.

5

Truth

We have been exploring the central element in Frege's philosophy–the thought, or sense of a sentence. Importantly, it is the thought that bears a truth-value. In other words, it is that which is said or expressed that is true or false. Thought is expressed to "get at the truth"; aiming at the truth is the primary function of the expression of thought. So we turn now to Frege's theory of truth.

What kind of thing is truth–a relation, a property or an object? And how exactly does truth relate to sentences and thoughts? As we shall see, Frege's conception of truth may be better understood against his general theory of sense and reference. What Frege argues is that a truth-value must be the reference of a sentence, and as such is determined by the sense of the sentence. But the sense of an expression determines an *object* as reference. What kind of object is "the true"? And why would it not be theoretically sound to understand truth as a relation or property?

Is Truth Relational?

What is truth? Traditionally it is thought of as a relation of correspondence between representations and the world. On this view a thought is said to be true when it corresponds with the world. A thought corresponds in this way when it is sufficiently similar to the thing it represents. We sometimes say that a painting is true when it accurately depicts a scene–that is, when it looks real. Similarly, treating a thought as a collection of ideas, we are led to believe that thoughts are true when they "look like" (or resemble enough) the part of the world that they represent.

Frege strenuously opposes any such correspondence theory of truth. His first criticism is that correspondence is a relation between two things (the representation and the thing that it represents), whereas application of the truth predicate, as in 'That sentence is true', never indicates a second thing with which the sentence is alleged to correspond. Frege writes,

> Is a picture considered as a mere visible and tangible thing really true, and a stone or a leaf not true? Obviously we could not call a picture true unless there were an intention involved. A picture is meant to represent something. (Even an idea is not called true in itself, but only with respect to an intention that the idea should correspond to something.) It might be supposed from this that truth consists in a correspondence of a picture to what it depicts. Now a correspondence is a relation. But this goes against the use of the world 'true', which is not a relative term and contains no indication of anything else to which something is to correspond. If I do not know that a picture is meant to represent Cologne Cathedral then I do not know what to compare the picture with in order to decide on its truth.[1]

The point here is this. Objects do not correspond on their own. There is no correspondence between things without the intent to have those two things correspond. A painting does not represent its object, unless it is intended to do so. Even a stone may represent something, but again, only if we intend it to do so. Without the intention to have them picture something, neither a stone nor a picture nor an idea will picture anything at all. Once it is recognized that correspondence presupposes the intent to have one thing represent another, one is committed to thinking that truth (as a relation of correspondence) is a relation between two things. Attributions of truth, on this theory, presuppose knowledge of at least two things: the representation and the thing represented. Such an account of truth would have us believe that truth is a two-place correspondence relation between a symbol and the thing it symbolizes. To say that x is true is then to say that x corresponds to something y. And yet, after being told that "x is true", we learn nothing about y. In particular, we do not learn what y is, so are ignorant of what x is supposed to correspond with. It seems that we may understand 'x is true' without ever knowing what y is supposed to be. But then 'x is true' cannot express a relation of correspondence between x and any other thing y.

More generally, a relation holds between at least two objects (or between an object and itself). By understanding a relational term in a sentence (as in 'Frege *is shorter than* Ludwig'), one knows of the objects being related (in this case, Frege and Ludwig). Otherwise, one is not grasping a relation when understanding the sentence. Since understanding a sentence of the form 'x is true' does not (for the general case) require one to grasp anything other than x (i.e., that which is said to be true) and the objects that x determines, it cannot be that truth is relational.

Of course, there is logical space to argue that truth is a relation between some one object and itself, just as the relation of identity relates an object to itself (as in, 'Superman *is identical to* Clark Kent'). But as Frege points out, a correspondence theorist cannot coherently adopt this reply. This would get the correspondence theorist around the problem of failing to grasp *two* objects while grasping the thought that something is true.

Frege notes that the correspondence theorist cannot avail himself of this solution. He notes that nothing *perfectly* corresponds with anything other than itself. This is because no object is similar to another object *in every respect*, unless it is that object. But since traditionally the correspondence theory claims that the truth of a thought (taken as a mental entity) consists in its corresponding with something other than itself (the world, in many cases, the physical world), correspondence cannot be between a thought and the world. As Frege puts it, "A correspondence ... can only be perfect if the corresponding things coincide and so just are not different things."[2] Frege goes on charitably to note that such strict correspondence

> is not at all what people intend when they define truth as the correspondence of an idea with something real. For in this case it is essential precisely that the reality shall be distinct from the idea. But then there can be no complete correspondence, no complete truth. So nothing at all would

be true; for what is only half true is untrue. Truth does not admit of more and less.[3]

The correspondence theorist traditionally argues that truth is a relation between an idea (or collection of ideas) and reality. Correspondence theories cannot then avoid Frege's first objection by adopting the view that the correspondence in question is a relation between an object and itself. The view is rather that the relation holds between distinct objects, ideas and the world. This reveals a second problem with correspondence theories; it requires that truth come in degrees.

As Frege points out in the above quote, perfect correspondence is impossible between distinct objects. So if two things correspond, it must be that they correspond to some degree. But this would be to say that truth admits of degrees–that '2 + 2 = 4' is true to some degree, just as the painting is an accurate depiction only to some degree. But it seems clear that '2 + 2 = 4' is either "fully" true or is false, and that there are no degrees of truth and falsity in between. A clear, unambiguous statement does not admit of more or less truth, but only is–or is not–true. Truth is an on-off feature; it is something a thought may be or fail to be. Correspondence, by contrast, (taken as a kind of similarity between distinct things) comes only in degrees.

So, truth is not correspondence with reality, because truth is not relational and because truth does not come in degrees.

Frege has a third criticism of the correspondence theory of truth. Even if correspondence could be defined as "correspondence in some particular respect" and this respect does not come in degrees, Frege believes there is an incoherence at the very heart of the correspondence theory of truth (or any relational theory of truth):

> ...could we not maintain that there is truth when there is correspondence in a certain respect? But which respect? For in that case what ought we to do so as to decide whether something is true? We should have to inquire whether it is *true* that an idea and a reality, say, correspond in the specified respect. And then we should be confronted by a question of the same kind, and the game could begin again.[4]

The idea seems to be this. If to say 'P is true' is to say

P corresponds (in some respect) to the world,

61

then we are confronted with a vicious regress. For we may always ask whether this new sentence is true. In other words, we may ask whether it is true that P corresponds to the world in this way. But on the correspondence theory, this amounts to asking whether

'P corresponds to the world' corresponds to the world.

Hence, we could not determine the truth of P until we have determined the truth of 'P corresponds in the relevant respect' (i.e., until we have determined that 'P corresponds in the relevant respect' corresponds to reality in the relevant respect). In the same way, we cannot determine that this latter claim is true until we have determined that

' 'P corresponds in the world' corresponds to the world' corresponds to the world.

And so on to infinity. To know whether P is true, we would have to verify an infinite number of other sentences. Since our finite minds are not capable of doing this, we could never determine the truth of a single issue.

A point of clarification is in order. Frege is not here worried about the following simple regress: if P is true, then it is true that P is true. And if it is true that P is true, then it is true that it is true that P is true...and so on. This regress by itself is not problematic. The problem arises when we equate truth with a relation such as "correspondence in the relevant respect". The problem arises here because seeking after truth becomes a matter of seeking the relevant relation between two things. Therefore, a precondition on verifying truth is that we verify that this relation obtains between the two things. But whether this relation really obtains (between the two things) is a question of whether it is *true* that this relation obtains. And a precondition on verifying this truth (that the relation really does obtain) is that we verify whether a new relation obtains–this time, between the world and the new claim, 'the relevant relation really does obtain between the two things'. To verify the truth of a single claim, in effect, requires that we verify the obtaining of an infinite number of relations–an impossible task for finite minds.

Is Truth Definable?

Frege's criticisms do not stop here. He makes a further subtle point that is supposed not only to go against the correspondence theory of truth but against *any* attempt to define truth. Frege explains,

> ... any other attempt to define truth also breaks down. For in a definition certain characteristics would have to be specified. And in application to any particular case the question would always arise whether it were *true* that the characteristics were present. So we should be going round in a circle. So it seems likely that the content of the world 'true' is *sui generis* [of its own kind] and indefinable.[5]

Notice that the criticism here appears not to be that a definition of truth creates an infinite regress, but that it would harbor some kind of *circularity*. Let us develop an understanding of the circularity in question.

The purpose of a definition is to give the meaning of a term. But a circular definition of a term provides something that presupposes an understanding of the term. In other words, if you cannot understand the definition without already understanding the term being defined, then the definition is circular. An extremely blatant violation might look something like this: a swabongo is something that looks and acts like a swabongo. This definition is clearly circular because one cannot understand the definition ('looks and acts like a swabongo') without understanding the term ('swabango') in advance. But then the meaning of 'swabongo' has not been provided. A definition that is circular is no definition at all, since the function of a definition is to elucidate meaning.

Now where lies the circularity in any definition of 'true'? Frege does not explain at length. So let us find some truth in his claim about the impossibility of defining 'true' for reasons having to do with circularity. Notice that a definition of 'true' will have to say when it is that something is true; it will have to say something of the following form: P is true *when and only when* A (where A is some given condition, such as 'P corresponds to reality' or 'P would be agreed to in ideal circumstances'). Whatever A happens to be, what will be said in the definition (at least implicitly) is that the expression on the left (i.e., 'P is true') is true in all and only those cases where the expression on

63

the right (i.e., 'A') is true. So, a definition of this form (perhaps, any definition of any expression) will presuppose an understanding of the very concept at the heart of our discussion, the concept of truth. For instance, to give the definition of 'bachelor' as 'unmarried male' we are perhaps implicitly saying that it is true that a thing is a bachelor in all and only those cases when it is true that the thing in question is an unmarried male. If that is what we are saying, then the definition presupposes an understanding of 'true'. In the case of 'bachelor' no circularity is apparent, since we do not need to understand 'bachelor' in order to understand 'unmarried male'—even if we do need implicitly to understand the notion of truth in order to understand the definition. But when 'true' is the very thing we are defining, the circularity is unavoidable. It is unavoidable since any definition providing the condition that must obtain for truth to obtain will require us (at least implicitly) to understand the expression 'the term on the left is true, when and only when the condition on the right is true'. For example, in 'P is true when and only when P corresponds with reality', one cannot say when and only when the condition on the right obtains without presupposing a sense in which it is *true* that that condition obtains. While defining truth, the circularity appears to be unavoidable. This must be the circularity that Frege has in mind when he claims that any definition of 'true' will be circular. If Frege is right, then truth is indefinable, or at least, it cannot be defined non-circularly in other terms. Truth is of its own kind.

Is Truth a Property?

If truth is not definable in other terms, then we must take it as a primitive notion. But without defining it, we may still inquire as to what kind of thing truth is. And if truth is not a relation between things, then what? At least grammatical 'is true' is a predicate, and so we might be led to think that truth is the property that 'is true' ascribes. To say 'P is true' would then be to attribute some property to P, just as saying 'The rose is red' is to attribute the property of being red to the rose. Frege considers this possibility:

> ...it is something worth thinking about that we cannot recognize a property of a thing without at the same time finding the thought *this thing has this property* to be true.

So with every property of a thing there is tied up a property of a thought, namely truth.[6]

If truth is a property then it is a peculiar one. For to notice that any thing has any property is to notice that truth applies. When I recognize that the rose is red, I notice not only that the rose has the property redness but also that the thought that the rose is red *is true*. The same may be said about the predication of any property of any object. Whenever we predicate something of an object, we are in effect predicating truth of the thought that contains that predication. Therefore, if truth is a property, it is one that applies whenever a property applies. Truth then is a peculiar property (if it is a property) because, unlike all others, it has this ubiquitous character of being present whenever properties of any kind are present.

Truth presents a further peculiarity, one that raises doubts about whether truth is a property at all.

It is also worth noticing that the sentence 'I smell the scent of violets' has just the same content as the sentence 'It is true that I smell the scent of violets'. So it seems, then, that nothing is added to the thought by my ascribing to it the property of truth.[7]

The claim here is that a sentence 'P' means exactly the same thing as 'P is true'. To say that P is to say no more and no less than that P is true. Consider Frege's test for sameness of content (discussed in Chapter 2): two thoughts are the same when and only when it is impossible to believe one without believing the other. It is impossible for you to believe that you smell violets unless you believe that it is true that you smell violets, and it is impossible for you to believe that it is true that you smell violets unless you believe that you smell violates. 'is true' then adds no further content to the thought of which it is predicated, and removing 'is true' from the predication withdraws no content from the original. 'is true' is semantically redundant.

For this reason, Frege finds it strange to think of truth as a property. Normally when we say that an object has a certain property, we are saying something substantial and informative. But when we say that a thought is true, we do little more than endorse the thought. 'is true' does not ascribe a substantial feature to the thought, and it does not say anything over and above what the thought already says. Frege is doubtful that truth is a property, but allows himself to talk "as if truth were a property, until some more appropriate way of speaking is found."[8] Nonetheless, in earlier writings we find a less ambivalent Frege. In *Sense and Reference* he argues that truth is no property at all, but rather is an *object*. We shall discuss this thesis further in the next section. Let us here review the ground we have covered.

What we have learned is that truth is *sui generis* (i.e., of its own kind) for three important reasons:

1. Truth cannot be defined (without circularity).

2. Truth is ascribed whenever a property is predicated of an object.

3. The truth-predicate 'is true' adds no further content by its application.

We have learned that truth cannot be treated as a relation or a property. It cannot be a relation because it is indefinable. Furthermore, relations hold between at least two objects. Competent use of the truth-predicate does not presupposes knowledge of two objects (as does the description of a correspondence between things), but only of the thing that is said to be true. Moreover, truth cannot be a property because the application of the truth-predicate is redundant (it adds no further content to the thing that it is applied to) and ubiquitous (it is implicit in the attribution of any property). In sum, the *sui generis* character of the truth precludes it from being either a relation or a property in the strict sense. But then what kind of thing is truth? Frege's answer may be better understood only after we have considered the role that truth plays in Frege's semantic theory.

The Reference of a Sentence

Consider again Frege's semantic categories of sense and reference. The sense is what is said or expressed by an expression, while the reference is that which the expression is about. In the last chapter we read that the sense of an assertoric sentence is a thought. What then is the reference of such a sentence? Do sentences have a reference?   And what is the semantic role played by truth?   These are the questions that we shall try to answer in this section.

Do sentences have a reference at all?   It depends:

> The fact that we concern ourselves at all about what is referred to by a part of the sentence indicates that we generally recognize and expect a reference for the sentence itself.   The thought loses value for us as soon as we recognize that the reference of one of its parts is missing. We are therefore justified in not being satisfied with the sense of a sentence, and in inquiring also as to its reference.[9]

Consider the sentence 'Frege died in 1925'.   Being concerned with the reference of 'Frege' (i.e., whom that term is about), we are naturally concerned with the reference of the sentence in which it appears.   That is, we are concerned with what 'Frege died in 1925' is about.   So we are interested not just in what it says (its sense), but the actual circumstance that it is about (its reference).   By contrast, consider the fictional sentence 'Gregor woke to find himself changed into a monstrous vermin'.   Since we know that Gregor does not really exist (the character is fictitious after all), the thought expressed lacks a certain value for us.   It lacks the value of determining some actual circumstance that the sentence literally depicts.[10]   So we do not seek a reference for a fictional sentence, even if we are intimately tied to its sense (what it says).   When a part of a sentence fails to have a standard reference, then so does the sentence of which it is a part.

The above discussion attempts to make the point in an informal way, that we seek the reference of a sentence whenever we seek a reference for its parts.   But notice that Frege puts forth the idea more formally in his compositionality thesis.   Recall that, on Frege's view, the reference of the whole is determined by the reference its parts.   In Frege's words,

> If we … replace one word of the sentence by another having the same reference, but a different sense, this can have no effect upon the reference of the sentence.[11]

'The Morning Star is the Evening Star' and 'The Morning Star is the Morning Star' must have the same reference, since their corresponding parts do.   Each proper name refers to the object which is Venus, so both sentences are about the relation of identity that holds between Venus and itself. In this way the reference of the whole sentence depends upon the reference of its parts (even if the two sentences do not share a sense). But now if a part of the sentence contains no reference, as with 'Gregor woke to find himself changed...', then the whole sentence does not have a reference. It does not have a reference, because the reference of the whole depends on the reference of the parts; and there are some missing parts. 'Gregor' does not have a reference, so neither does any sentence for which 'Gregor' is used as the subject. For these formal and informal reasons Frege claims that

> ... the reference of a sentence may always be sought, whenever the reference of its components is involved.[12]

But what exactly does Frege take the reference of a sentence to be? Well, what is the relevant difference between a referring and a non-referring sentences? Consider: 'Frege died in 1925' and 'Gregor woke to find himself changed into a monstrous vermin'. What is it that we are seeking of the former but not of the latter? Frege answers,

> [we seek the reference of the components and so the reference of the whole sentence] if and only if we ask for the truth-value.[13]

Allegedly, we seek the truth when and only when we seek reference. We care about the actual objects and so the circumstance of which they are a part, just in case we are interested in the truth or falsity of the sentence that depicts them. So given that an interest in reference always coincides with an interest in the truth-value of the sentence, Frege believes that the truth-value of a sentence (either the value true or the value false) *is* the reference of the sentence. We seek one whenever we are seeking the other, so it is reasonable to suppose that they are one and the same.

The test for whether this is right is to apply Frege's principle of the compositionality of reference:

> If our supposition that the reference of a sentence is its truth-value is correct, the latter must remain unchanged when a part of the sentence is replaced by an expression with the same reference. And this is in fact the case.[14]

According to the compositionality principle, when we take a sentence and replace one of its terms with another term having the same reference, the reference of the whole sentence remains the same. Under such substitutions, the sense of the sentence will often be changed, but the truth-value stays the same. If we substitute 'Morning Star' for 'Evening Star' in 'The Evening Star is Venus', we get 'The Morning Star is Venus'. The sense of the sentences changes, yet the truth-value remains unchanged.

Moreover, by Frege's lights, there is nothing semantically relevant other than truth-value that satisfies this referential compositionality principle:

> If we are dealing with sentences for which the reference of their component parts is at all relevant, then what feature except the truth-value can be found that belongs to such sentences quite generally and remains unchanged by substitutions of the kind just mentioned?[15]

Frege suggests that the only thing that remains unchanged across substitutions of co-referring terms is the truth-value of the sentence. Truth-value is the only semantic element that is preserved when we substitute constituent terms for others having the same reference. Therefore, it must be the case that the reference of a sentence is its truth-value.

Is Truth an Object?

We return now to our inquiry about the nature of truth. Frege has argued that the truth-predicate–'x is true'–does not express a property or a relation, despite its grammatical similarity to expressions that express properties and despite its traditional treatment as a relational of correspondence. If truth is not a property or relation, then what is it? Apparently, there is only one other kind of thing that truth may be–an object.

> We are … driven into accepting the *truth-value* of a sentence as constituting what it refers to. By the truth-value of a sentence I understand the circumstance that it is true or false.

There are no further truth-values. For brevity I call the one the True, the other the False. Every assertoric sentence concerned with what its words refer to is therefore to be regarded as a proper name, and its reference, if it has one, is either the True or the False. These two objects are recognized, if only implicitly, by everybody who judges something to be true....[16]

When I assert 'Frege died in 1925', I say something about Frege. The sentence is about (or refers to) the obtaining of a certain circumstance. Recall that a proper name expresses a sense and denotes an object. The assertoric sentence is treated here like a proper name. The sentence expresses a sense and names an object. It expresses a thought, and names the True (or the False).

Frege's use of the word 'circumstance' may cause some confusion here. When he says that 'The rose is red' names the circumstance that it is true, Frege does not intend to say that it names the circumstance, or state of affairs, that consists of the rose's being red. The sentence *expresses the thought* that the rose is red, but it, like all true statements, names an object–the True. Hence, all true sentences name the same object. All false sentences, analogously, name the same object–the False.[17]

It is a peculiar consequence that all true sentences name the same object, the True. The peculiarity is especially evident when we realize that, for Frege, the reference of an expression is what the expression is about. All true statements are then about the same thing! Frege hopes that this consequence will not be too disturbing once it is recognized that co-referring sentences may *say* distinct things. That is, they express distinct thoughts, even if they name the same object. The relevant difference between, say, 'Roses are red' and 'Violets are blue' may then be explained by their difference in sense. And as Frege points out, when seeking the truth, *both* sense and reference are essential:

> If now the truth-value of a sentence is its reference, then on the one hand all true sentences have the same reference and so, on the other hand, do all false sentences. From this we see that in the reference of the sentence all that is specific is obliterated. We can never be concerned only with the reference of a sentence; but again the mere thought alone

yields no knowledge, but only the thought together with its reference, i.e., its truth-value.

Sense without the reference is what we often find in fictional discourse. The names, and so the sentences, do not always refer to actual objects. But that is just fine, since fictional sentences are not in the business of making claims to truth. That is why we call them fictional. So, in assertoric discourse, where one is making judgments in an effort to get at the truth, one is not interested in the sense alone. Neither is one ever interested in the reference of a sentence (what the sentence is about), unless one is also interested in what the sentence says. So the fact that all true sentences are about the same thing does not make a relevant difference, even if it does require us to part from the standard use of the term 'about'.

Just as the sense of a name determines an object as reference, so too the sense of a sentence (the thought) determines an object (the value True, or the value False) as reference. In fact, on this semantic theory, a sentence just is a kind of name, hence functions as one.

In the second chapter we discovered that the sense of a proper name is, for Frege, its "mode of determination"—its criterion for determining an object (its reference). What we now learn is that a sentence is a kind of name that expresses a thought which in turn acts as a way of determining a reference for that sentence, True or False.

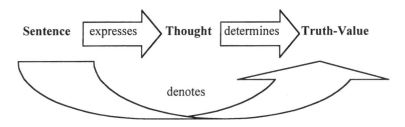

The thought is that part of the meaning of a sentence that determines a truth-value, in much the same way that the sense of a name is that part of its meaning that determines an object. The thought is true or false in virtue of the thought's structure, so the structure of a thought may be treated as a way in which a truth-value is determined.

Endnotes

[1] Thoughts, 59-60.

[2] Thoughts, 60.

[3] Thoughts, 60.

[4] Thoughts, 60.

[5] Thoughts, 60.

[6] Thoughts, 61.

[7] Thoughts, 61.

[8] Thoughts, 62.

[9] Sense and Reference, 33.

[10] These remarks are not meant to suggest that fictional sentences have no value, but merely to mark a difference between the role fictional discourse plays in contrast with assertoric discourse. Even if fictional sentences are about actual circumstances in a metaphorical sense, they are not literally so. They do not make literal claims to truth, and are not treated as candidates for truth in the relevant respect.

[11] Sense and Reference, 32.

[12] Sense and Reference, 34.

[13] Sense and Reference, 34.

[14] Sense and Reference, 35.

[15] Sense and Reference, 35. In the same place, Frege credits this principle of compositionality to Leibniz.

[16] Sense and Reference, 34.

[17] The following might be suggested: since the reference of the sentence is a function of the references of its constituent parts, the object that is the rose and the concept red are "parts" of the True. But so are the objects and functions denoted by the parts of any true sentence. 'Frege died in 25' denotes the True, and so, the object that is Frege and the concept referred to by "died in 1925" are also parts of the True. Frege is not happy with this talk of "parts" of a truth-value, since the reference of 'Frege died in 25' (i.e., the True) minus the reference of 'Frege' does not leave us with the remainder (i.e., the reference of 'x died in 25'). But admittedly not having a better way of speaking, Frege

cautiously allows himself the freedom of this way of speaking. See Sense and Reference, 35-36.

6
Intensional Contexts

In "Sense and Reference" Frege foreshadows an objection to his thesis that the truth-value of a sentence is its reference. For it appears that in certain contexts one may substitute co-referring expressions without preserving truth-value. If this is right and the reference of a whole sentence is a function of the reference of constituent parts, then arguably the reference of a whole sentence is not its truth-value. This chapter is dedicated to Frege's solution of this puzzle. The solution resolves the apparent inconsistency in adopting both the compositionality thesis and the claim that sentences denote truth-values.

The issue becomes apparent only after it is emphasized that whole sentences can themselves be parts of more complex sentences. Consider,

(1) Grass is green and snow is white.

This compound sentence contains two simple sentences as parts. 'Grass is green' and 'Snow is white' are both true. In virtue of this and the way that 'and' functions, the entire conjunction is true (or names the True, as Frege would say). So if we replace one of the more basic sentences with another having the same reference (i.e., the same truth-value), the reference (truth-value) of the compound sentence should be preserved. And it is. Replace the true sentence 'Grass is green' with the true sentence 'Whales are mammals'. We obtain

(1*) Whales are mammals and snow is white.

This new compound sentence is true. (1*) does then have the same reference as (1), since both are true. We obtain the same results when substituting in for co-referring constituent sentences of any conjunction. Moreover, truth-value is preserved when substituting in for constituent sentences of other compound sentences, such as disjunctions, conditionals and negations.[1] The proof is left to the reader as an exercise. What we learn is that the replacement of co-referring sentences within a variety of compound sentence structures can be performed *salva veritate* (while preserving truth).

Of course, the above examples are not the exceptional cases, but instead only further confirm Frege's general claim that the compositionally determined reference of a sentence is its truth-value. The puzzle arises in cases of what Frege calls *indirect speech*. Consider the following sentences:

(2) Columbus thought that he sailed to India.

(3) Lois is certain that Superman can fly.

(4) Rudolf believes that the Morning Star is Venus.

These are examples of "indirect speech" because the thoughts expressed by the component sentences (namely, 'Columbus sailed to India', 'Superman can fly', and 'the Morning Star is Venus') are being attributed rather than expressed directly by the person who utters (2), (3) or (4), respectively.

The problem is that when we substitute these component sentences with others having the same truth-value, we sometimes fail to preserve the truth-value of the whole. Sentence (2) is true, but its component sentence 'Columbus sailed to India' is false. Replace this false sentence with another that is false, say, 'Columbus sailed to Antarctica', to get

(2*) Columbus thought that he sailed to Antarctica.

This new sentence (2*), unlike (2), is false, even though we replaced a component sentence in (2) with one having the same truth-value. We exchanged co-referring component sentences without preserving the truth-value of the whole. Even if we simply replace one name with another having the same reference, we fail to preserve truth-value for the general case. Replace 'Superman' with 'Clark Kent', since they refer to the same thing, and similarly 'the Morning Star' with 'the Evening Star'. The outcomes of these substitutions are the following sentences.

(3*) Lois is certain that Clark Kent can fly.

(4*) Rudolf believes that the Evening Star is Venus.

In cases where (3) and (4) are true, (3*) and (4*) may be false. For Lois may not know Superman's true identity, and Rudolf may be unaware that the Morning Star is the Evening Star. Since we have only replaced co-referring terms, doubts are raised about Frege's thesis that the compositionally determined reference of a sentence is its truth-value. Doubts are raised, because we have replaced terms with others having the same reference, yet the truth-value of the sentence is not preserved. If the truth-value of a sentence were determined by the reference of its constituent parts, then sameness of reference among the parts should preserve sameness of reference for the whole. But then if the reference of a whole sentence is determined by the references of its parts, it is not clear that the reference of a whole sentence is its truth-value.

Today philosophers say that such component sentences appear *in opaque contexts*, so called because the truth-value of the whole sentence is not preserved under a substitution of co-referring parts. Such contexts are sometimes called *intensional contexts*. One type of intensional context is created by the attribution of mental (or intentional) states. Intensional contexts have similar logical forms:

x believes that P
x knows that P
x is certain that P
x desires that P
x can doubt whether P,

Where 'x' is the name of a person and 'P' is a sentence. These are also called "propositional attitude ascriptions", since asserting a sentence of this form is to ascribe to someone a thought that is the object of their psychological attitude.

Propositional attitude ascriptions are logically problematic, because they do not function like other truth-evaluable sentences. We have already seen that they fail to satisfy the compositionality principle. Failure to recognize this has led even eminent thinkers down fallacious paths of reasoning. For example, we are usually able to infer that an object b has a certain property F, if $a = b$ and a has property F:

> Object a has property F
> $a = b$
> Therefore, object b has property F

This is a valid form of inference, but only when considering premises whose truth-values are determined by the reference of more basic parts. Without realizing this, one may be led to make the following inference.

> Superman is known by Lois to fly.
> Superman = Clark Kent
> Therefore, Clark Kent is known by Lois to fly.

Of course, if Lois does not know Superman's identity, then she does not know that Clark Kent can fly. It is fallacious to suppose that such a conclusion follows in intensional contexts–hence the name of this mistaken inference form, *the intensional fallacy*.[2]

One version of Descartes' argument for dualism commits this fallacy. Dualism is the thesis that says mind and body are two very different kinds of things, that mind and body are composed of distinct kinds of matter. Descartes argued that the mind cannot be part of the body, since it is possible to doubt that you have a body but not possible to doubt that you have a mind. His famous slogan, "I think therefore I am" is meant to encapsulate the idea that as long as you are thinking, nothing could be more certain than that you exist–as a mind! By contrast, your body may be an illusion. It is possible that you are right now dreaming, and merely appear to have this body before you. Since you can doubt that you have a body but not that you have a mind, mind is not identical to body.[3]

This argument presupposes that if mind and body were identical and you could *doubt* the existence of one, then you could doubt the existence of the other. This reasoning matches the argument form discussed above. Since this argument essentially involves reports about one's own doubts, the argument commits the intensional fallacy.

Frege explains why the compositionality of reference fails in intensional contexts. It fails because the component sentences do not have their usual reference. When we say that Lois believes that Superman can fly, our report is not strictly speaking about Superman. We are not asserting the truth or falsity of anything about Superman. Our report is about Lois's attitude and the content of her attitude. We are referring to Lois's *thought* that Superman can fly.

> In indirect speech, words are used *indirectly* or have their *indirect* reference. We distinguish accordingly the *customary* from the *indirect* reference of a word.... The indirect reference of a word is accordingly its customary sense. Such exceptions must always be borne in mind if the mode of connection between sign, sense, and reference in particular cases is to be correctly understood.[4]

So it seems that the reference of a sentence is not always its truth-value, and the referents of constituent proper names are not always objects. In intensional contexts (or indirect speech), the reference of a component sentence will be its customary sense–that is, the thought that it would normally express, were it not embedded in a propositional attitude context. The reference of a name appearing in such embedded sentences will be the sense that is normally expressed by that name in its customary use, were it not embedded in a propositional attitude context.

Letting the arrows signify relations of reference, Frege's standard model of a sentence and the referential relations that it stands in may be represented in the following way:

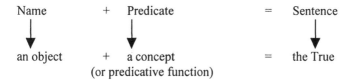

78

In the special case where that very sentence appears in an intensional context, Frege describes a different model (again, letting arrows signify referential relations):

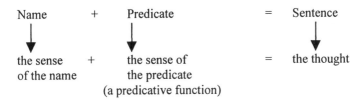

Name   +   Predicate   =   Sentence

the sense   +   the sense of   =   the thought
of the name   the predicate
                   (a predicative function)

Since the truth-value of the component sentence is not the reference of that sentence, it is no surprise that its truth-value does not figure in a determination of the truth-value of the propositional attitude ascription. The solution to the puzzle is to continue to embrace the compositionality principle and the principle claiming that a complete sentence denotes a truth-value, as long as one realizes that in intensional contexts there may be component sentences that do not play their customary referential role. In such contexts an embedded sentence may be about the thought that it normally expresses, rather than the truth-value that it normally denotes.

Endnotes

[1] *Disjunctions* are statements of the form 'p or q', *conditionals* of the form 'if p then q', and *negations* 'it is not the case that p'–where 'p' and 'q' stand for more basic sentences that have a truth-value, true or false.

[2] Today it is strange to think of "being known by Lois to fly" as a property. Considerations about intensionality have led philosophers to conclude as much.

[3] Descartes' fallacious argument may be found in the Sixth Meditation of his *Meditations on First Philosophy*.

[4] Sense and Reference, 28.

7
Logic

In *The Foundations of Arithmetic* Frege issues several warnings to philosophers investigating questions of meaning.[1] Among them:

> always separate sharply the psychological from the logical, the subjective from the objective.

> never ask for the meaning of a word in isolation, but only in the context of a proposition.

The first warning is never to confuse the psychological with the logical. What is the logical? Apparently, to confuse the psychological with the logical is to confuse the subjective with the objective. So "the logical" is that part of meaning which is objective. But how are we better to understand the connection between objective meaning (sense) and logic? That is the question at hand, and throughout this chapter.

The Context Principle

Frege's second warning, known today as *the context principle*, is never to investigate the meaning of a term independently of the sentence in which it appears. If one does, then

One is almost forced to take as the meanings of words mental pictures or acts of the individual mind, and so to offend against the first principle as well.[2]

The suggestion is that if we consider the meaning of 'rose' and 'red', for instance, in isolation from the sentences in which they appear, it will be all too easy to equate their meanings with the ideas we associate with them. Considering the meaning of 'red' in isolation, I call to mind a faint visual image of the color red. One might suppose that that image just is the meaning of 'red'. But as we discussed in the chapter on thought, the image I have of 'rose' plus the image I have of 'red' is not sufficient to explain the meaning of 'The rose is red'. More specifically a combination of subjective states cannot explain the objectivity of thought. To explain the objectivity of thought one must be able to say how it is that several people may grasp and communicate the same thought, and how a single person may grasp the same thought at different times. Moreover, a combination of ideas cannot explain the truth-evaluable nature of thought. Thoughts are capable of being true or false, but it is a complete mystery as to how images may combine to create something capable of being true or false. This becomes especially apparent once it is realized that truth cannot be treated as a relation of correspondence between images and the things they are said to correspond to. The context principle is in effect warning us not to make this mistake of equating meanings with psychological entities, for fear of confusing the subjective with the objective.

The context principle would rather have us ask first for the meaning (the sense) of the whole sentence. When we begin there, we do not lose sight of what needs to be explained: the communicability and truth-evaluability of meaning. For it is the whole sentence that allows us to communicate and express something capable of being true or false. The thought, for Frege, is that thing which is communicated and assessed for truth or falsity. In a further investigation of meaning, one which asks for the meanings of the terms appearing in a sentence, the task then becomes to locate that part of the term's meaning which contributes to this special character of thoughts. Frege's theory of sense aspires to do just that. The sense of a subject term (taken as argument) and the sense of a predicate term (taken as a function) give rise to the truth-evaluable nature of thoughts. Moreover, since a thought determines its truth-value, we may understand the sense of a term as follows. The sense of a term is the contribution it makes to determining the truth-value of the whole thought of which it is a part. The sense of a name, for example, contributes by providing a way of picking out an object. The sense of a predicate-expression contributes by picking out a concept or predicative function. Each of these senses plays a role in determining the truth or falsity of the thought of which they are a part. In sum, senses combine to explain the truth-evaluability of thought, and to determine the truth or falsity of the thought. Failing to recognize that which needs to be explained, perhaps by not heeding the warning of the context principle, one may be misled into providing a psychological account of meaning.

There is a second explanation for why philosophers were often led to psychological theories of meaning. Thoughts, like ideas, are not perceivable objects. We do not turn our senses to the physical world in order to grasp either a thought or an idea. Given this similarity, one may hastily conclude that a thought is psychological in nature. But as we have learned, thoughts are objective, mind-independent and truth-evaluable. Psychological entities, such as ideas, are not. It is this failure to recognize that something objective may not be detectable by the senses, perhaps, that leads one to a psychological theory of meaning. The question of objectivity is not the question of whether something is physical, or detectable by the senses. All things that are detectable by the senses are objective, but not all things objective are detectable by the senses.

Thoughts (unlike mental entities but like physical entities) are objective, and (unlike most physical objects but like mental entities) are not detectable by the senses. Since thoughts exist neither in the realm of the physical nor in the realm of the mental, Frege notices,

A third realm must be recognized.[3]

Thoughts are said to occupy this third order of reality–an order that is distinct from the physical and psychological orders. To recognize this in our investigation of meaning is to separate sharply the subjective from the objective. But why is this also to separate the psychological from the *logical*? What does logic have to do with the study of objective thought?

What is Logic?

Frege's conception of logic is the one we have today, since it is the one we have adopted from him. The task of logic is to answer questions about what thoughts follows from what other thoughts, and so to establish which truths may be inferred from other truths.

> To establish laws of inference is the task of logic.[4]

> To make a judgement because we are cognizant of other truths as providing a justification for it is known as *inferring*. There are laws governing this kind of justification, and to set up these laws of valid inference is the goal of logic.[5]

Logic is the study of justified inference–the study of what we may infer to be true, given that others things are true. For instance, given that a conjunction is true, we may infer each of its conjuncts. So from the truth of "Frege was a mathematician, and Frege was a philosopher" we may infer "Frege was a mathematician". More generally,

> Given that 'P and Q' is true, one may infer 'Q'.

'P and Q' is a justification for inferring 'Q'. 'Q' is justified, because it is a consequence of the conjunction, 'P and Q'. If the conjunction 'P and Q' is true, then 'Q' is true as well. We are led then to the very obvious law of inference above. Let us take another example. Given that a conditional is true and that its antecedent is true, we may infer its consequent. So from the truth of 'If I am in Vienna, then I am in Austria' and the truth of 'I am in Vienna' we may infer that it is true that I am in Austria.

> Given the truth of 'If P then Q' and the truth of 'P', one may infer 'Q'.

'If P then Q' and 'P' jointly provide a justification for inferring 'Q', because 'Q' is a consequence of that pair of sentences.

Notice that these are *laws* of inference, because they are perfectly general. One may substitute any sentence one likes for 'P' and any sentence one likes for 'Q', and the inference will remain valid. Given that grass is green and snow is white, one may infer that snow is white.

Given that 4 is the sum of two primes and 4 is even, one may infer that 4 is even. So the laws of logic are applicable for all regions of rational discourse. As Frege puts it,

> [The laws of logic] are the most general laws, which prescribe universally the way in which one ought to think if one is to think at all.[6]

The laws of logic are "most general" in that they describe what follows from what *in any region of rational discourse.* They hold in mathematics, physics, biology, archeology, philosophy, everyday discourse, etc. And, for that very reason, they are "universal" in that they prescribe how *anyone* is to think, if he/she is to think at all. Because the laws of logic are perfectly general (i.e., describe what truths follow from what truths, in any region of discourse), Frege calls these laws 'the laws of truth'. And because they issue universal demands on how we should think, he calls them 'the laws of thought'. We will consider each of these ideas in turn, so as to elucidate further Frege's conception of logic.

The Laws of Truth

Logic is the study of what truths follow from other truths. Its task is to establish laws of inference based upon this study. For this reason, Frege tells us,

> Our conception of the laws of logic is ... connected with our understanding of the word "true".[7]

> It would not perhaps be beside the mark to say that the laws of logic are nothing other than an unfolding of the content of the word 'true'. Anyone who has failed to grasp the meaning of this word–what marks it off from others–cannot attain to any clear idea of what the task of logic is.[8]

> The task of logic being what it is, it follows that we must turn our backs on anything that is not necessary for setting up the laws of inference. In particular we must reject all

85

distinctions in logic that are made from a purely psychological standpoint and have no bearing on inference.[9]

Given that the essential task of logic is to uncover the laws of inferring truths from other truths, the study of logic should focus upon only those features of inference that are relevant to the preservation of truth.

An inference consists of the judgment that some conclusion is true, based on the judgment that some premises are true. A judgment is the endorsement of a thought. A thought, as we have learned, is true or false independently of anyone's endorsement of it. The only things relevant to determining the truth of a thought are the senses of which it is composed. A thought determines its own truth or falsity in virtue of its internal structure. A conjunction 'P and Q', for instance, is true or false in virtue of its function/argument structure. It is true just as long as we plug into the function

$$(\ ) \text{ and } (\ )$$

conjuncts that are both true. In other words, a conjunctive thought is true when and only when its component parts (those expressed by 'P' and 'Q') are both true. These component parts are true, depending on their internal function/argument structure. If 'P' says 'Frege was a mathematician', then the truth-value is determined by the sense expressed by 'Frege' and the function expressed by 'was a mathematician'. Together they compose a thought that is true given the object determined by the sense of 'Frege' and the concept determined by the sense of 'was a mathematician'.

Sense, according to Frege, is all that is necessary for setting up the laws of logic, because sense is all that is relevant for determining truth. Once we grasp the sense of the conjunction, we know under what conditions it is true. It is true just in case both conjuncts are true. But then we know that if the conjunction 'P and Q' is true, so is 'P'. The law of truth that we may establish is this: given the truth of 'P and Q', 'P' is true, or from the truth of 'P and Q' one may infer 'P'.

Sense turns out to be that part of meaning that is necessary and sufficient for logical inference. And sense, we have learned, is objective in that it is intersubjectively graspable and mind-independent. It is in this sense, then, that an investigation of meaning that fails to separate sharply the subjective from the objective amounts to a failure to separate the psychological from the logical.

The Laws of Thought

The laws of logic were called the 'laws of thought' by Frege and his predecessors. But

> the expression 'laws of thought' seduces us into supposing that these laws govern thinking in the same way as laws of nature govern events in the external world.[10]

Laws of nature *describe* ways in which nature behaves. Laws of thought are not meant to describe ways in which we happen to think, not if laws of thought are to be equated with laws of logic. For the laws of logic are meant to *prescribe* how one ought to think.

> Only in the latter sense can the laws of logic be called 'laws of thought': so far as they stipulate the way in which one ought to think.[11]

Logic then is not only to be understood as providing the laws of truth, generalizations about what truths follow from what truths, but as prescribing how one ought to think if one is interested in attaining truth. In this sense only, according to Frege, laws of logic are to be understood as laws of thought. But many of his contemporaries were seduced into treating laws of logic as descriptions of how people do in fact think. Frege dedicated himself to proving, once and for all, that such a psychological treatment of logic must be wrong since it undermine the very possibility of meaningful discourse.

Anti-Psychologism

The view that logic is a branch of psychology has come to be called *psychologism*. The laws of logic are said on this view to be empirical generalizations of human thinking. These laws then depend fundamentally on the ways in which we do reason. The important consequence of psychologism is this: if we were to reason differently

87

from the ways we do in fact reason, then the laws of logic would be other than they happen to be. Here is Frege's version of the insight:

> if logic were concerned with these psychological laws it would be a part of psychology; it is in fact viewed in just this way. These laws of thought can in that case be regarded as guiding principles in the sense that they give an average, like statements about 'how it is that good digestion occurs in man', or 'how one speaks grammatically', or 'how one dresses fashionably'. Then one can only say: men's taking something to be true conforms on the average to these laws, at present and relative to our knowledge of men; thus if one wishes to correspond with the average one will conform to these. But just as what is fashionable in dress at the moment will shortly be fashionable no longer and among the Chinese is not fashionable now, so these psychological laws of thought can be laid down only with restrictions on their authority. Of course–if logic has to do with something's being taken to be true, rather than with its being true! And these are what the psychological logicians confuse.[12]

So if psychologism is true and the laws of logic just are the laws of human thinking (in the sense that they describe how humans do in fact think on average), then logic loses its universal authority. For the laws of logic (statements about which truths follow from other truths), are reduced to statements about what humans take to be true in light of other things that they take to be true. Since humans may change their minds about what follows from what, the laws of logic may change. Moreover, since different humans do think differently, the laws of logic are different for different people. The laws of logic then do not prescribe universally how one is to think if one is to think at all, but at best only prescribe how one is to think if one is to think like the average member of that community at that time.

The problem, as it will turn out, is that if logic is relative to how communities happen to think here and now, then it can no longer be used to evaluate our judgments for correctness, even here and now. Because of this it undermines the very possibility of meaningful discourse. Our local goal is to clarify these Fregean insights.

Let us suppose, for the sake of argument, that psychologism is true–that the laws of logic are contingent on the ways humans do think. Now consider the law of logic known as *modus ponens*. It says,

'if P then Q' and 'P' jointly entail 'Q'.

We normally think in accordance with this law. For instance, if we think 'If it is snowing then it is cold' and we think 'It is snowing', then we infer that it is cold. When we think 'If I miss the final exam then I will fail the course' and think 'I missed the final', then we conclude 'I will fail the course'–and so on, for all substitution-instances of *modus ponens*. If the psychological logician is right, then these pieces of reasoning are not *universally* valid. That argument form does not have a mind-independent validity, since the validity of that argument form does not precede our reasoning in accordance with it. Instead, our reasoning that way makes the argument form valid. First we reason in a certain way and–in virtue of our so doing–the form of that reasoning becomes good. So, if we did not reason from a conditional and its antecedent to its consequent, then *modus ponens* would not be valid.

> Accordingly, the possibility remains of men or other beings being discovered who were capable of bringing off judgments contradicting our laws of logic. ...But what if beings were ... found whose laws of thought flatly contradicted ours and therefore frequently led to contrary results even in practice? The psychological logician could only acknowledge the fact and say simply: those laws hold for them, these laws hold for us. I should say: we have here a hitherto unknown type of madness. Anyone who understands laws of logic to be laws that prescribe the way in which one ought to think–to be laws of truth, and not natural laws of human beings' taking a thing to be true–will ask, who is right? Whose laws of taking-to-be-true are in accord with the laws of truth? The psychological logician cannot ask this question; if he did he would be recognizing laws of truth that were not laws of psychology.[13]

We reason in accord with *modus ponens*. The other beings reason not according to *modus ponens*, but instead according to *modus schmonens*: from 'If P then Q' and 'P' they infer 'Not-P'. They accuse us of

89

fallacious reasoning. Of course, they reason according to principles that we find fallacious. One wonders whether there is an objective way to resolve this logical disagreement. So Frege asks, who is right? Whose logic is correct? As he notes, the psychological logician cannot make sense of the question, since psychological logic is just a set of generalizations about how communities of people do think. We think one way, they think another. To suppose there is a question of correct thinking over and above these facts, is to deny psychologism. It is to admit that logic does not merely describe how we think, but prescribes how one ought to think independently of how one's community happens to think. To admit that there is an issue of correctness is to admit that there are extra-psychological laws of logic. But again, this is simply to undermine psychologism.

Of course the psychological logician must deny that there is an issue of correctness between logically divergent communities. Our differences do not, strictly speaking, present a contradiction. Our psychological law says that we think one way, and their law says that they think another way. This is no more a contradiction than generalizations about how we and they fashionably dress. We dress this way; they dress another way. Who is correct, we or they? The question does not make sense. There are ways that one must dress to dress fashionably in one community, and ways that one must dress to dress fashionably in another. There are no principles of fashion over and above those that emerge *within* the community. Fashion is relative—so too is logic, if psychologism is true. Issues of correct versus incorrect inference do not arise between communities.

When issues of correctness do not arise, however, neither does the possibility of agreement or disagreement. As we discussed in the chapter on thoughts, a genuine disagreement between thinkers presupposes the possibility that at least one of them is in error. If issues of correctness and incorrectness do not arise between two communities, then it is not possible for speakers from different communities to have a real disagreement. Moreover, there is no clear sense in which thinkers from different communities may be in agreement. To claim that our judgements are in agreement presupposes that there is something that it would be for them to be in disagreement. We "would not be able to assert anything at all in the normal sense", since we would not be able to express anything capable of standing in relations of affirmation and denial. We legitimately conclude that P, and they legitimately conclude that not-P. If the latter is not really the denial of former, then we do not mean the same thing by 'P'. We cannot communicate at all.

Importantly, if thinkers from different logical communities cannot communicate, then there is no clear sense in which speakers of the same community can communicate. For if people think differently, the psychological logician is forced to admit that the laws of logic are different for different people. And there would be no question of who is correct, since on this psychological view there are no laws of logic over and above those that describe how people do in fact think. But then speakers within the same community would not be able to agree or disagree in any logically relevant sense. There would be nothing that one person may affirm and another denies. They could not share a point of contention at all. But then they could not communicate. At best they could vent their own subjective states. Such ventings would more closely resemble interjections than assertions. Just as the interjection 'Yummy' does not allow anyone else to grasp the speaker's sensation of delight, the utterance of a declarative sentence would not allow anyone else to grasp the speaker's meaning. They would not be able to communicate anything capable of being true or false. Natural language, on the psychological account of logic, is itself a mere series of meaningless grunts and groans. Noises without content!

Since rational discourse is possible, and we are able to agree, disagree and communicate meaning, psychologism is false. The laws of logic are not mind-dependent. If they were, we would not be able to communicate and share the contents of our utterances. A theory of logic that fails to separate the psychological from the logical in effect confuses the subjective with the objective. It reduces the publicly accessible content of our utterances to incommunicable states of an individual mind.

Conclusion

Let us summarize the ground we have covered. Two main principles motivate much of Frege's philosophy of meaning. First there is the *compositionality principle*, which most generally says that the objective meaning of a whole sentence is a function of the meanings of its constituent parts. So if we replace a term in a sentence with another having the same meaning, then the remaining sentence will have the same meaning as the original sentence. Second, there is Frege's *principle for the individuation of meaning*–a principle for determining whether meaning P and meaning Q are one and the same meaning. P and Q are one and the same when and only when it is impossible to believe P without believing Q and impossible to believe Q without believing P. Accordingly, if I may believe that Superman can fly without believing that Clark Kent can fly, then 'Superman can fly' and 'Clark Kent can fly' do not share a meaning. Frege used these principles together to show that there must be more to the meaning of an expression than reference. For given the compositionality of reference, 'Superman can fly' and 'Clark Kent can fly' have the same reference (since 'Superman' and 'Clark Kent' refer to the same thing and 'can fly' refers to the same thing in each of its occurrences). Nevertheless, there is a sense in which these two sentences have different meanings, since they fail to test for sameness of meaning. This puzzle led Frege to adopt his semantic dualism: objective meaning is to be divided into sense and reference. The sense of an expression is what is said, and the reference is that which the sentence is about. 'Superman can fly' and 'Clark Kent can fly' share a reference but not a sense. They are about the same thing, since they are both about Superman. But they do not say the same thing since one can understand both sentences while taking the former, but not the latter, to be true. Objective meaning, it seems, must be understood in terms of both sense and reference. Frege's defense of the sense-reference distinction was the primary concern of Chapter 2.

In the third chapter on objectivity we discussed the basic difference between the subjective and the objective, and presented Frege's view about the objectivity of sense. Ideas are quintessentially subjective because they are private and mind-dependent. A sense, by contrast, is publicly accessible, and depends for its existence on no particular mind. This position was developed further in Chapter 4, in terms of the objectivity of thought, where a thought is taken as the sense of a whole sentence. A thought, like any sense, is objective in that it is publicly accessible and mind-independent. Thoughts are a special kind of sense, because they are capable of truth or falsity. They are the primary bearers of truth-value. Thoughts also have internal structure in virtue of which they have this special status. Moreover, it is the internal structure of thought that determines which truth-value is had. Consequently, thoughts are objective in a further respect. Since the truth-value of a thought is determined by its internal structure, thoughts are true or false independently of the subjects who judge; the truth of a thought is independent of our taking it to be true. If truth-value were not independent of judgment in this way, there would not be any possibility of mistaken judgment. And this would undermine the very possibility of rational discourse, which includes the possibility of meaningful disagreement, the evaluation of opinion, and of communication more generally–all of which presuppose the possibility of mistake and contradiction in judgment. Our utterances would not express anything at all in the normal sense, since on this view what is expressed would not stand in the appropriate logical relations required for normal rational discourse. At best, our utterances would amount to a mere evincing of internal states, just as 'yuck' says nothing literally but instead serves to express the speaker's disgust. In sum, the truth of a thought is independent of our taking it to be true; otherwise that which is expressed by an utterance could not be intersubjectively graspable, communicable or truth-evaluable. If truth were mind-dependent, rational discourse would be impossible.

In the final chapter on logic we said that an essential task of logic is to determine which truths follow from which other truths, and so to determine which truths we may infer from other truths. Facts about what follows from what justify our inferences. If we judge that the road is wet upon learning that it is raining, then we would be justified in so judging (since we also believe that if it is raining, the road is wet). Others would be correct in agreeing with us. On the other hand, if we judge that it is raining upon learning that the road is wet, we would not necessarily be justified (even if we believe that if it rains, the road is wet). We would not be justified on this basis alone, since the roads may have been dowsed in some other way–possibly by the sprinklers, possibly by the street cleaners, possibly by some other means. Others would be correct in questioning our judgment that it has rained, lacking further information. In a word, logic makes rational discourse possible. It provides the tools for evaluating judgment. It provides the means by which we may have a coherent and productive agreement or disagreement.

In that same chapter we evaluated Frege's insight that a confusion of the logical with the psychological amounts to a confusion of the objective with the subjective. The reason for this is that the confusion of logical laws with psychological laws reduces differences of objective meaning (for instance, the difference between a thought and its negation) to mere subjective differences (such as the difference between what is expressed by your 'Yum!' and my 'Yuck'). Logical difference, on the psychological account, is treated as a species of psychological difference. The problem is that once logic is treated psychologically, we lose the objectivity of thought that is inherent to rational discourse. Recall that sense is that part of meaning that is relevant to logical inference–that part of meaning relevant for the evaluation of judgment. The sense of an expression is the contribution it makes to determining the truth-value of sentences in which that expression appears. The sense of a sentence (a thought) is then the contribution it makes to determining the truth-value of that and related sentences. Logic aims to determine which truths follow from which truths, and for this reason, logic is the study of thought. To confuse logic with psychology is to confuse the study of thought with study of ideas. It is to confuse the objective with the subjective, and so to undermine the possibility of rational discourse.

If it makes sense to engage in rational discourse, then it seems we need a theory of objective meaning–we need a theory of sense. But there is a tension in the theory. Frege's theory of sense relies importantly on his criterion for the individuation of meaning, which says that thought P and thought Q are one and the same thought, when and only when it is impossible to believe one without believing the other. Notice the appeal to psychological states of belief. Does this not make the sameness of meaning a mind-dependent phenomenon? Sameness of meaning after all turns on what can or cannot be believed. Frege's theory then appears to hinge on considerations about what can or cannot be done with the human mind. Does Frege's theory of sense ultimately rest on such psychological considerations? If so, then Frege's theory of logic turns out to be a species of the very psychologism that he believes undermines the possibility of logic.

The problem may be put another way. Does Frege's criterion of identity for meanings commit an intensional fallacy? We analyzed this fallacy in Chapter 6. Remember that identical things a and b share all the same features, unless those features are intensional in nature. That is, identical things are not necessarily objects of the same psychological attitudes. Lois believes that Superman can fly and Superman is identical to Kent, but it does not follow that Lois believes that Kent can fly. For she may not know that Superman is Kent. One might think that Frege is committing a version of this fallacy, since his criterion for identity of meaning appears to involve the following inference:

It is believed that P

P = Q

Therefore, it is believed that Q

If this inference were valid, then it would be clear that if it is believed that P but not believed that Q, then P is not identical to Q. But of course, as it stands, this inference appears to be invalid, since, one might argue, belief that P and the identity of P with Q is not enough to guarantee the belief that Q. After all, does not one need to know further that P is the same as Q?

The tension in Frege's theory may be resolved. The problem lies in thinking that the above inference is what motivates Frege's criterion of identity. Frege's criterion says that meaning P and meaning Q are the same just as long as *it is impossible* to believe one without believing the other. Frege's criterion would be motivated by an intensional fallacy, if the notion of possibility here were interpreted as a kind of psychological possibility. But now that we have a better grasp of Frege's notion of objective meaning, we need not understand this notion of possibility psychologically. Sense is the relevant part of meaning in question. And sense is that part of meaning that is relevant to logical inference. We might better understand this notion of possibility in logical, rather than psychological, terms.

What Frege has in mind then is the question of what we are *justified* in believing:

> P and Q are one and the same thought when and only when it is impossible to be justified in believing one without being justified in believing the other.

And the kind of justification in question is logical justification. So,

> P and Q are one and the same thought when and only when, P logically implies Q, and Q logically implies P,

where 'logical implication' is a matter of which truths necessarily follows from other truths, *independently of what we may or may not take to be true*. In logic books today we call this 'logical equivalence'. The following two sentences express logically equivalent thoughts:

I have neither time nor money.

and,

I do not have time, and I do not have money.

These sentences express the same sense, because they are interderivable by logical means. The former implies the latter, and conversely. *As a result*, it is logically impossible to believe one without believing the other. That is, if P is logically justified then so is Q, and vice versa. Logically speaking they say the same thing, since it is impossible to be logically justified in believing one without being logically justified in believing the other. By contrast, 'Superman can fly' does not logically imply 'Kent can fly'. One may be justified in accepting the former without being justified in accepting the latter. Logically speaking they do not say the same thing. They do not have the same sense.

Frege's test for sameness of meaning does not, then, depend on psychological considerations and does not harbor an intensional fallacy. This becomes clear once we understand that sense is that part of meaning relevant to logical inference, and accordingly rethink Frege's test in purely logical terms. The appeal to belief is eliminable in a proper characterization of Frege's test for sameness of sense.

What have we learned about the metaphysical nature of sense, of logical content, of thought? Frege does not offer a positive account of the underlying nature of thought, and philosophers today are still grappling with the issue. So we will not attempt to answer that question here. In Frege's later writings we find a hint of mysticism. We will close then on an enigmatic note about the metaphysical nature of sense. Logic is the study of objective meaning; it the study of thought. Its task is to investigate the internal structures of thoughts and to establish the laws of inference that they determine. Since our grasp of thoughts is not a perceptual process, thought does not exist in the physical realm. And since a thought is objective and mind-independent, it cannot have a psychological nature either. Frege tells us that "a third realm must be recognized". Thoughts occupy this realm. This realm is the special subject matter of logic.

> Neither logic [the study of thought] nor mathematics [a special extension of logic] has the task of investigating minds and contents of consciousness owned by individual men. Their task could perhaps be represented rather as the investigation of *the* mind; of *the* mind, not of minds.[14]

Logic then is the study of *the* mind, a third order of reality distinct from the physical and psychological orders. It is the task of logic to map its terrain: to describe the truth-value relevant structure of thought, and so, to establish the relations (or logical consequences) among thoughts. Frege discovered and charted the structure of the third realm in his first book, *Begriffschrift*. Perhaps better to understand the metaphysical nature of thought, we must also see into this realm. Fortunately, we need only pick up a logic book to explore its exotic landscapes.

Endnotes

[1] *The Foundations of Arithmetic*, J. L. Austin (tr.), 2nd ed., Northwestern University Press, 1980, p. x.

[2] Ibid.

[3] Thoughts, 69.

[4] Logic (between 1879 and 1891), in H. Hermes, F. Kambartel and F. Kaulbach (eds.), *Posthumous Writings*, University of Chicago Press, 1979, p. 2.

[5] Ibid., p. 3.

[6] *The Basic Laws of Arithmetic*, M. Furth (trans. and ed.), University of California Press, 1967, xv.

[7] *The Basic Laws of Arithmetic*, xiv-xv.

[8] Logic (between 1879 and 1891), op. cit., p. 3.

[9] Ibid., p. 5.

[10] *The Basic Laws of Arithmetic*, xv.

[11] *The Basic Laws of Arithmetic*, xv.

[12] *The Basic Laws of Arithmetic*, xv.

[13] *The Basic Laws of Arithmetic*, xvi.

[14] Thoughts, 74.